Better Homes and Gardens®

Cooking
FOR
One

Our seal assures you that every recipe in *Cooking for One*
has been tested in the Better Homes and Gardens® Test Kitchen.
This means that each recipe is practical and reliable, and
meets our high standards of taste appeal.

BETTER HOMES AND GARDENS® BOOKS
Editor: Gerald M. Knox
Art Director: Ernest Shelton
Managing Editor: David A. Kirchner
Editorial Project Managers: James D. Blume, Marsha Jahns,
    Rosanne Weber Mattson, Mary Helen Schiltz

Department Head, Cook Books: Sharyl Heiken
Associate Department Heads: Sandra Granseth,
    Rosemary C. Hutchinson, Elizabeth Woolever
Senior Food Editors: Julia Malloy, Marcia Stanley, Joyce Trollope
Associate Food Editors: Linda Henry, Mary Major, Diana McMillen,
    Mary Jo Plutt, Maureen Powers, Martha Schiel,
    Linda Foley Woodrum
Test Kitchen: Director, Sharon Stilwell; Photo Studio Director,
    Janet Pittman; Home Economists: Lynn Blanchard, Jean Brekke,
    Kay Cargill, Marilyn Cornelius, Jennifer Darling,
    Maryellyn Krantz, Lynelle Munn, Dianna Nolin, Marge Steenson

Associate Art Directors: Linda Ford Vermie, Neoma Alt West,
    Randall Yontz
Assistant Art Directors: Lynda Haupert, Harijs Priekulis,
    Tom Wegner
Senior Graphic Designers: Jack Murphy, Darla Whipple-Frain
Graphic Designers: Mike Burns, Sally Cooper, Brian Wignall
Art Production: Director, John Berg; Associate, Joe Heuer;
    Office Manager, Emma Rediger

President, Book Group: Fred Stines
Vice President, Retail Marketing: Jamie Martin
Vice President, Direct Marketing: Arthur Heydendael

BETTER HOMES AND GARDENS® MAGAZINE
Vice President, Editorial Director: Doris Eby
Executive Director, Editorial Services: Duane L. Gregg
Food and Nutrition Editor: Nancy Byal

COOKING FOR ONE
Contributing Editors: Barbara Thornton Associates
Editorial Project Manager: Marsha Jahns
Graphic Designer: Sally Cooper
Electronic Text Processor: Joyce Wasson
Contributing Food Stylists: Suzanne Finley, Maria Rolandelli
Contributing Photographers: Michael Jensen and Sean Fitzgerald

On the front cover: Florentine Lasagna Rosettes
(see recipe, page 48)

When Better Homes and Gardens® asked me to be the contributing editor for a cookbook entitled *Cooking for One,* it was a welcome and exciting challenge.

We began our research by inviting a group of people who cook for themselves to a discussion dinner meeting. This group included women of all ages. We also consulted with several men who cook for themselves. These lively discussions inspired recipe ideas and tips.

All of the people we talked with told us they often skip breakfast. In our "Morning Meals" chapter we included blender drinks and Breakfast Sandwiches to Go for people with busy schedules. Many of the recipes in the "Light Meals" chapter also make hearty snacks. In this chapter we created soups and salads, and used tortillas in fun ways. In "The Rest of the Meal" chapter, we developed several basic recipes that can be prepared in various ways. For example, the Basic Refrigerator Bran Muffin Batter can be used for a muffin, but with the addition of simple ingredients this same batter can be used to make four desserts.

If you were entertaining a VIP, you probably would prepare something special. Well, you are special, too, and you deserve the very best meals. The recipes in this cookbook are delicious, attractive, and easy to prepare. Start cooking for someone special—*you.*

Barbara Thornton

Your Kitchen for One

A well-stocked and well-organized kitchen will help you spend less time and effort preparing food. These pages contain hints for shopping, equipping your kitchen, stocking your shelves, and storing foods.

Shopping Wisely

When you push that grocery cart through the store, you're enjoying one of the benefits of cooking for one. You can buy exactly what *you* want.

But you also have the challenge of satisfying yourself when it comes to cooking and eating. It all starts *before* you get to the supermarket. Start to plan for the days ahead. Read the ads in the newspaper and check your pantry and refrigerator. See Cook Once, Enjoy Twice on page 73 for menu planning help.

Think of the arrangement in your favorite grocery store when you write your shopping list. Plan your list to match your route through the store.

In the grocery store, take extra time to look for new products, especially single-serving products. Ask the butcher at the meat counter for individual portions. Visit the deli. You can purchase many of the ingredients in our recipes in small quantities.

Some stores even have salad bars where you can purchase small quantities of vegetables for salads or stir-frying.

Watch for items that will fit on your "emergency shelf" (see page 76). If you keep a few items handy, you can have a meal ready in minutes.

Remember, a bargain is not a bargain if you can't use it all. Buy only amounts you can handle easily. Think small.

Finally, check the hints on page 9 for storing the foods you've just purchased.

Here is a sample of the kind of list you may want to use.

SHOPPING-FOR-ONE LIST

Produce
vegetables: _____

_____

fruits: _____

_____

Dairy
milk: _____
margarine/butter: _____
cheese: _____
yogurt: _____
eggs: _____

_____

Meat
bacon: _____
beef: _____
pork: _____
chicken: _____
fish: _____

_____

_____

Frozen Foods

_____

_____

_____

Canned Foods

_____

_____

_____

Staples

_____

_____

_____

Baking Supplies

_____

_____

_____

Deli

_____

_____

_____

Bakery

_____

_____

_____

Snacks

_____

_____

Beverages

_____

_____

Household

_____

_____

Personal

_____

_____

Other

_____

_____

_____

Selecting Equipment

The right kitchen equipment in the right place can make cooking a breeze. Begin with some good basic equipment, and as space and budget permit, add some of the fun gadgets that make cooking easier and faster. Store items that you use less often in out-of-the way areas and keep the most-used items in convenient spots.

BASIC EQUIPMENT USED IN COOKING-FOR-ONE RECIPES

For recipe preparation:
Glass measuring cup
Set of nested dry measuring cups and measuring spoons
Mixing bowls
Wooden spoons
Slotted spoon
Pancake turner
Rubber scrapers
Tongs
Ladle
Sharp knives
Vegetable peeler
Kitchen scissors
Can and bottle openers
Wire whisk
Rotary beater and/or electric mixer
Colander
Strainer
Pastry brush
Grater
Cutting board
Kitchen scale

For range-top cooking, baking, and broiling:
6- or 8-inch skillet with nonstick surface
Large saucepan (for pasta)
1- and 1½-quart saucepans
Teakettle
Vegetable steamer basket
Baking sheet
Small casseroles (10 to 24 ounces)
6-ounce custard cups
Small loaf pans, pie plate, and tube pan
Cooling racks
Roasting pan with rack
Small broiler pan

Your Kitchen for One

Stocking Shelves

In addition to your favorite packaged, canned, and frozen foods, keep a supply of these basic foods on hand. As storage space and budget permit, add extra items according to personal preference.

SHELF STAPLES
Basic ingredients:
All-purpose flour
Sugars—granulated, brown, and powdered
Baking powder
Baking soda
Cooking oil, shortening
Salt, pepper
Vanilla, other flavorings
Dried herbs
Spices
Unsweetened cocoa powder
Catsup, mustard
Vinegar
Worcestershire sauce
Soy sauce
Steak sauce
Rice, pasta
Cereals
Bread *or* cracker crumbs

Nice to have:
Coffee, tea, beverage mixes
Salad dressings
Instant chicken *or* beef bouillon granules
Semisweet chocolate pieces
Raisins, other dried fruits
Jam, jelly
Peanut butter
Condiments, relishes
Salsa
Evaporated milk
Packaged mixes
Canned fruits, vegetables

REFRIGERATOR STAPLES
Basic ingredients:
Margarine *or* butter
Mayonnaise *or* salad dressing
Eggs
Milk
Cheese
Fruits, vegetables
Juices

Nice to have:
Dairy sour cream, yogurt
Fresh gingerroot
Grated Parmesan cheese

FREEZER STAPLES
Basic ingredients:
Meat, brown-and-serve sausage
Frozen fruits, vegetables
English muffins, other breads

Nice to have:
Tortillas
Cranberries
Puff pastry dough

NONFOOD ITEMS
Wooden toothpicks, skewers
Clear plastic wrap
Foil
Reclosable plastic bags
Nonstick spray coating

Storing Foods

Food storage is the vital link between buying the food and eating the meals. Storing food is especially important for the person cooking for one because it may take longer to use up items. This information will help you store food properly to keep it at its best.

SHELF STAPLES (65°-70°F)

Cereals, croutons, dry bread crumbs: Store in airtight containers (away from heat sources such as your range, exhaust vent, refrigerator, or under-cabinet lighting). Check dates on packages. For best flavor, use within 3 to 6 months from date of purchase.

Pasta, rice: Store in airtight containers. Keep for up to 2 years.

Canned goods: For best quality, use within 1 year. Discard any can with leaks or bulges.

Seasonings, herbs, spices: Store, tightly closed, in a dry, dimly lit place, such as inside a cupboard. (Sunlight can reduce flavor and aroma.) Check flavor at least once a year; replace as needed.

IN REFRIGERATOR (35°-40°F)

Dairy products:
Milk or cream, 3 to 7 days
Margarine, 1 month
Butter, 1 to 2 weeks
Soft cheeses, 1 week
Hard cheeses, 1 month
Eggs, 2 weeks

Meats, poultry, and fish: Store ground meats, poultry, and fish in the coldest area and use within 1 to 2 days (freeze, if you need to store longer). Store other meats in coldest area and use within 2 to 4 days.

Fruits: Strawberries and ripe peaches or pears should be used within 3 to 5 days. Use apples within 1 month. Use citrus fruits within 2 weeks.

Vegetables: Use spinach, lettuce, and all leafy greens within 5 days. Cabbage, celery, and carrots will keep for up to 2 weeks.

Other foods: Store cooking oil, nuts, ground coffee, syrup, jam, and peanut butter in the refrigerator to retain flavor and freshness.

IN FREEZER (0°F)

Store foods for shorter times if your freezer does not maintain a temperature this low. Wrap in moisture- and vaporproof materials such as freezer paper or heavy foil, or use freezer containers.

Dairy products:
Soft cheeses, 1 month
Hard cheeses, 2 months (texture may be crumbly; thaw in the refrigerator)
Margarine or butter, 3 to 6 months

Meats, poultry, and fish:
Beef, 6 to 12 months
Pork, 3 to 6 months
Ground meats, 3 months
Poultry, 6 months
Bacon and frankfurters, 1 month
Cooked meats, 2 to 3 months

Fruits and vegetables: Use within 8 to 12 months for best quality.

Cooked foods, leftovers:
Casseroles, 2 to 3 months
Soups, 6 months
Sandwiches, 2 weeks (do not freeze mayonnaise)

Morning Meals

Start your day
with one of our Morning Meals. It can
be yogurt mixed with your
favorite cereal, a sandwich to eat on
the go, or a weekend omelet.
Choose a recipe to fit your pace.

An Egg—The Most Natural Single Portion

Many stores sell eggs in bulk or in half-dozen quantities. Keep eggs in the covered egg carton in the refrigerator for up to 2 weeks.

Don't limit eggs to just Morning Meals; egg dishes are appealing for any meal. A Mexican Quiche or a Vegetable Frittata is ideal for brunch, lunch, or any light meal.

Egg dishes are versatile. Change the flavor of a basic omelet with different fillings. When a child comes to visit, serve Egg in a Basket, or treat the kid in you anytime.

Breads—An Endless Variety

Enhance your Morning Meals by using a variety of breads. Breakfast Sandwiches to Go were created using popular bakery breads. We discovered you *can* purchase items individually—a croissant, a bagel, a scone, or a baking powder biscuit. Some bakeries even sell half-loaves of bread to accommodate the person cooking in small quantities. The Egg in a Basket and French Toast for One recipes will work with several breads—French, white, whole wheat, or cinnamon.

Wrap slices of bread, English muffins, and rolls individually and store them in the freezer for up to 2 months so they will be fresh and handy when needed.

Fresh Fruit Blender Drink

A morning blender drink, fresh with fruit and tangy with yogurt.

1 **cup sliced fresh** *or* **frozen fruit**
1 **6- to 8-ounce carton vanilla yogurt**
½ **cup milk**
1 **tablespoon honey** *or* **sugar (optional)**

● In a blender container combine fruit, yogurt, milk, and honey; cover and blend well. Garnish with a strawberry, if desired. Makes 1 serving.

Orange Juice Special

Blend orange juice concentrate with yogurt and an egg for a special breakfast drink.

1 **6- to 8-ounce carton vanilla yogurt**
1 **egg**
3 **tablespoons frozen orange** *or* **tangerine juice concentrate**
½ **teaspoon honey**
1 **ice cube (optional)**

● In a blender container combine yogurt, egg, orange juice concentrate, honey, and ice cube, if desired; cover and blend well. Garnish with an orange slice, if desired. Makes 1 serving.

Anytime Eggnog

A delicious breakfast drink good any day of the year.

1 **ripe small banana**
1 **egg**
½ **cup milk** *or* **light cream**
Dash ground nutmeg
Drop of vanilla *or* **rum extract**

● In a blender container combine banana, egg, milk or cream, nutmeg, and vanilla or rum extract; cover and blend well. Garnish with banana slice, if desired. Makes 1 serving.

Blender Beverages

You can make any of these blender drinks ahead and chill for up to 1 hour. For a frosty dessert, prepare and freeze a blender beverage for 1 hour before serving.

Orange Juice Special

Fresh Fruit Blender Drink

Anytime Eggnog

Breakfast Yogurt

For variety use your favorite cereal, fruit, and vanilla or other flavored yogurt in this nutritious and easy breakfast.

1 6- to 8-ounce carton vanilla *or* other flavored yogurt
½ small apple, cored and diced (¼ cup)
1 tablespoon quick-cooking rolled oats
1 tablespoon raisin bran cereal

● In a small bowl combine yogurt, apple, rolled oats, and raisin bran cereal. Cover and chill for 30 minutes. (Breakfast yogurt can be prepared the night before and left in the refrigerator overnight.) Makes 1 serving.

Hard-Cooked Egg Supreme

If you like Eggs Benedict, you'll like this convenient, lower-in-calories brunch dish.

3 fresh mushrooms, sliced
1 tablespoon margarine *or* butter
1 tablespoon all-purpose flour
Dash Worcestershire sauce
Dash salt
Dash pepper
¾ cup milk
2 tablespoons shredded Swiss cheese
1 hard-cooked egg, sliced
1 English muffin, split and toasted
2 tablespoons cooked bacon pieces
1 teaspoon diced pimiento (optional)
Fresh fruit (optional)

● In a small saucepan cook mushrooms in margarine or butter till tender. Stir in flour, Worcestershire sauce, salt, and pepper till blended. Add milk all at once. Cook and stir till thickened and bubbly, then cook and stir for 1 minute more.

● Add cheese and stir till melted. Gently stir in egg slices. Cover and cook for 1 to 2 minutes longer or till egg is heated through.

● Spoon over toasted English muffin. Top with bacon pieces. If desired, garnish with pimiento and serve with fresh fruit. Makes 1 serving.

Vegetable Frittata

A frittata is an open-faced Italian omelet.

1 tablespoon margarine *or*
    butter
¼ cup sliced fresh mushrooms
1 whole tiny new potato,
    thinly sliced
1 green onion, sliced
2 eggs, beaten
2 tablespoons milk
¼ teaspoon dried basil,
    crushed
⅛ teaspoon salt
    Dash pepper
¼ cup shredded herb-flavored
    cheese *or* Swiss cheese
2 cherry tomatoes, quartered

● In a 6-inch skillet melt margarine or butter. Add mushrooms, potatoes, and green onion. Cook over medium heat till potato is tender, turning occasionally.

● Meanwhile, in a small bowl combine eggs, milk, basil, salt, and pepper. Pour egg mixture into skillet. Cook about 2 minutes or till the egg mixture is set, running a spatula around edge of skillet and lifting mixture to allow uncooked portion to run underneath. Remove from heat. Top with cheese and tomatoes. Makes 1 serving.

Lifting edge of frittata
As the egg mixture begins to set around the edge and changes from wet-shiny to dull, run a spatula around the edge of the skillet, lifting the frittata to allow the uncooked eggs to run underneath. This helps to cook the eggs evenly.

Mexican Quiche

Mexican Quiche

This quiche is Mexican all the way—a tortilla crust and a filling of favorite "south of the border" flavors.

1 6-inch flour tortilla
½ cup shredded Monterey
    Jack cheese (2 ounces)
3 ounces bulk pork sausage
1 tablespoon chopped green
    pepper
1 egg
¼ cup milk *or* light cream
⅛ teaspoon salt
    Hot salsa (optional)
    Fresh cilantro (optional)

● Starting with a cold skillet, heat tortilla about 45 seconds or till warm, turning once. Place tortilla into a greased 15-ounce casserole. Top with ¼ *cup* of the cheese.

● In same skillet cook sausage and green pepper till sausage is cooked and green pepper is crisp-tender; drain well. Spoon over tortilla and cheese in casserole.

● In a small bowl combine egg, milk or cream, and salt. Mix well. Pour egg mixture into casserole. Top with remaining cheese. Bake in a 350° oven for 30 to 35 minutes or till firm. Serve with hot salsa and cilantro, if desired. Makes 1 serving.

Raisin Bran Pancakes

This hearty pancake is made from a refrigerator bran batter. In "The Rest of the Meal" chapter, there are five convenient recipes that use this batter.

⅓ cup Basic Refrigerator Bran
    Muffin Batter (see recipe,
    page 90)
1 tablespoon milk
1 teaspoon margarine *or*
    butter
    Maple-flavored syrup

● In a small bowl combine batter and milk till well blended.

● In an 8-inch skillet melt margarine or butter over medium heat. Add half of the batter mixture to the skillet and cook about 2 minutes or till underside is light brown. Turn; cook about 1 minute more or till pancake is done. Repeat with remaining batter. Serve with maple-flavored syrup. Makes 1 serving.

French Toast for One

French bread (¾ to 1 inch thick) is especially good, but you may use any sliced bread or sandwich rolls.

1 **egg, slightly beaten**
¼ **cup milk *or* light cream**
2 **slices bread**
1 **tablespoon margarine *or* butter**
   Maple-flavored syrup
   Fresh fruit (optional)

● In a small shallow flat dish beat together egg and milk or cream with a fork till combined. Dip bread slices in egg mixture. In a medium skillet melt margarine over medium-low heat.

● Cook dipped bread slices in margarine for 2 to 3 minutes on *each* side or till golden brown. Serve with maple-flavored syrup. Garnish with fresh fruit, if desired. Makes 1 serving.

Savory French Toast: Prepare French Toast for One as directed above, *except* add 1 teaspoon chopped *onion,* ⅛ teaspoon dried *dillweed,* and dash *pepper* to egg mixture. If desired, top cooked slices with shredded *cheese.*

Orange Dessert Toast: Prepare French Toast for One as directed above, *except* add 1 teaspoon *sugar,* ¼ teaspoon finely shredded *orange peel,* and a few drops of *vanilla* to the egg mixture. If desired, sift *powdered sugar* over cooked slices.

Note: To make ahead, place bread slices in egg mixture, cover tightly, and refrigerate overnight. Or, dip bread slices in egg mixture, wrap individually in moisture- and vaporproof material, and freeze for up to 1 week. Cook as directed.

Egg in a Basket

When you're in a hurry, omit the egg mixture for dipping. Simply butter bread generously on both sides and brown in a skillet.

1 slice white, whole wheat, *or* raisin bread
2 eggs
1 tablespoon milk
   Dash salt
   Dash pepper
1 tablespoon margarine *or* butter
1 slice Swiss *or* other cheese
   Avocado slice (optional)
   Tomato slice (optional)

● Cut a hole 2½ or 3 inches in diameter from the center of bread slice. Reserve center round. In a small shallow flat dish combine 1 of the eggs, milk, salt, and pepper. Dip bread slice and center round in egg mixture.

● In a medium skillet melt margarine or butter over medium heat. Cook dipped bread slice and center round in margarine about 1 minute on each side or till light golden brown. Drop remaining egg in center of slice and cook till egg is almost of desired doneness. Turn over and top with cheese. Cook about 1 minute more or till cheese is slightly melted. (For an egg cooked sunny-side up, cook for 2 minutes, and cover skillet after adding cheese slice.) Garnish with avocado and tomato slices, if desired. Makes 1 serving.

Putting the egg in the slice of bread
Crack the egg and gently drop egg into hole in the browned slice of bread. When egg is almost cooked to desired doneness, turn over and top with a slice of your favorite cheese.

Breakfast Sandwiches to Go

Fast food restaurants have made breakfast sandwiches popular. To make your own, mix and match the following breads and fillings. Let your appetite and imagination be your guides. Just add fruit and a glass of milk to complete the meal.

Strawberry-Filled Croissant

Split a *croissant;* spread bottom half generously with *soft-style cream cheese.* Spread with *strawberry preserves,* then assemble. If sandwich is made ahead, store it in the refrigerator.

Peanut Butter-Banana Sandwich

Use 2 slices of *cinnamon, whole wheat, or raisin bread;* spread 1 slice with *peanut butter.* Sprinkle with cooked *bacon pieces,* then assemble. If sandwich is made ahead, store it in the refrigerator. Before serving, add ½ *banana,* sliced.

Breakfast Pita

Cut a *pita round* in half crosswise. Combine 1 tablespoon dairy *sour cream* and ⅛ teaspoon prepared *mustard.* Spread *half* inside pita halves. Combine remaining sour cream mixture and 1 chopped *hard-cooked egg.* Season to taste. Line each pita half with 1 thin slice of fully cooked *ham* and fill with egg mixture.

If desired, heat pita halves. To heat in the microwave, loosely wrap pita halves in clear plastic wrap. Micro-cook on 100% power (high) about 45 seconds. To heat in the oven, wrap pita halves in foil and heat in a 350° oven about 15 minutes.

Peanut Butter-Banana Sandwich

Cheese-Filled Bagel

Egg-and-Sausage Scone

Split a *scone or baking powder biscuit*. Place 1 cooked brown-and-serve *sausage patty* and 1 scrambled *egg* on bottom half. Top with 1 tablespoon *applesauce,* then assemble.

If desired, heat sandwich. To heat in the microwave, loosely wrap sandwich in clear plastic wrap. Micro-cook on 100% power (high) about 45 seconds or till sausage is warm. To heat in the oven, wrap sandwich in foil and heat in a 350° oven about 18 minutes.

Cheese-Filled Bagel

Split a *bagel* (any flavor); spread bottom half with 2 tablespoons *soft-style cream cheese*. Sprinkle with 2 tablespoons finely chopped fully cooked *ham or* cooked *bacon pieces*, then assemble.

How to Hard-Cook Eggs:

Place eggs in a small saucepan; cover with cold water. Bring to boiling; reduce heat to just below simmering. Cover and cook for 15 minutes. Remove from heat. Run cold water over eggs till cool. Remove shells; chop or slice eggs.

Egg-and-Sausage Scone

Breakfast Pita

Strawberry-Filled Croissant

21

Uses for Leftover Food

No one likes dibs and dabs of food in the refrigerator or pantry, so in creating these recipes for one serving, we tried to use the whole piece or package of the ingredient. Generally, we were successful, but sometimes a small amount is left. Here are some creative uses for those leftover amounts of food.

Alfalfa sprouts	Use instead of lettuce as a base for salads or sandwiches.
Avocado	Add to sandwiches or salads, or mash and spread on toast (to store after cutting, leave seed in, skin on; wrap tightly and refrigerate for up to 2 days).
Bean dip	Add to salads or sandwiches, or spread on tortilla chips.
Bread crumbs	Use as a meat coating, casserole topper, or meatball ingredient.
Coconut	Sprinkle on fruit ambrosia, puddings, or curry dishes, or toast for ice cream topping.
Cream cheese	Spread on bagels or use in dips, sandwich spreads, or dessert tarts.
Eggs	Hard-cooked: use for garnishes or salads, or in white sauce over toast. Yolks: use in pots de crème, puddings, custards, or scrambled eggs. Whites: use in desserts, soufflés, sherbets, or macaroons.
Gingerroot	Grate and add to marinades, salad dressings, or fruit compotes, or grate for stir-fries (store gingerroot in brandy or sherry in a small jar in the refrigerator).
Mushrooms	Add to salads, soups, white sauce, sandwiches, or omelets (cook fresh mushrooms and freeze).
Olives	Use in salads or sandwich fillings, or for garnishes or pizza topping.
Pimiento	Add color to casseroles, cream sauces, or sandwich fillings.
Potatoes, cooked	Use in frittatas, hash, or soups, or marinate for salads.
Spinach	Use in salads, omelets, quiches, or soups, or serve creamed over toast.
Vegetables	Use cold in salads, or add to soups, casseroles, or stir-fries.
Wheat germ	Add to cereals, stir into yogurt, or add a little to batters or doughs when baking (store in the refrigerator).
Yogurt	Combine with chopped fruit and nuts or combine with whipped cream and freeze for desserts.

Omelet for One

An omelet makes a light meal morning, noon, or night. Simply add your favorite filling.

2 eggs
2 teaspoons water
⅛ teaspoon seasoned salt *or* salt
    Dash dried marjoram *or* thyme, crushed, *or* fines herbes
    Dash pepper
2 teaspoons margarine *or* butter

● Beat together eggs, water, salt, herb, and pepper with a fork till combined but not frothy. In a 6- or 8-inch skillet with flared sides, heat the margarine or butter till it sizzles.

● Lift and tilt the pan to coat the sides. Add egg mixture; cook over medium heat. As egg mixture sets, run a narrow spatula around the edge of the skillet, lifting the egg mixture to allow uncooked portion to flow underneath. When egg is set but still shiny, remove from heat. Fold omelet in half. Slide omelet from the skillet onto a warm plate. Makes 1 serving.

Veggie-Filled Omelet: Cook ⅓ cup sliced fresh *mushrooms,* ¼ cup *broccoli flowerets,* and 2 tablespoons chopped *onion* in 2 teaspoons *margarine or butter* till tender; keep warm. Prepare Omelet for One as directed above, *except* fill omelet with vegetable mixture before folding it in half.

Cheesy Omelet: Prepare Omelet for One as directed above, *except* fill omelet with 2 tablespoons shredded *cheddar or Monterey Jack cheese* and 1 ounce *cream cheese,* cut into ½-inch cubes, before folding it in half. Sprinkle with 2 tablespoons additional shredded cheese and snipped *parsley,* if desired.

Elegant Seafood Omelet: Cook ½ cup chopped *spinach* and one 1-ounce crab-flavored *fish stick,* chopped (¼ cup), in 2 teaspoons *margarine or butter* till fish is heated through; keep warm. Prepare Omelet for One as directed above, *except* fill omelet with spinach mixture and ¼ cup shredded *Swiss cheese* before folding it in half.

Tomato-and Pastrami-Filled Omelet: Prepare Omelet for One as directed above, *except* fill omelet with ¼ cup chopped *pastrami, cooked turkey, or fully cooked ham* before folding it in half. Top with ¼ cup chopped *tomato.*

Light Meals

Light Meals
can be lunches, dinners, or snacks.
You decide if you want a tempting
salad, a different sandwich idea, a
satisfying soup, or a new tostada recipe.
They're all quick and easy to prepare.

Think Deli

More and more grocery stores feature deli departments. A tremendous help for people cooking for themselves, delis offer both convenience and variety. And you can purchase just the amount of food you want.

You can use many deli items in several ways. For example, three or four slices of turkey pastrami will be enough for a sandwich and an omelet filling, too. A small amount of coleslaw will yield enough for a sandwich filling as well as a side dish. Creamy fruit salad can be a filling for a cookie tart and it can top a slice of cake. You can purchase the new crab-flavored fish sticks individually for salads, creamed seafood, or an omelet filling, or for topping a microwave-cooked fish fillet.

Tostada—A Light Meal

The dictionary defines *tostada* as a tortilla that is fried till crisp. Many restaurants offer a crisp tortilla topped with shredded lettuce, seasoned meat, chopped tomato, sour cream, and shredded cheese and call it a tostada. We have created some new versions of the tostada.

Tortillas, corn or flour, are similar to pizza crust and offer an infinite variety of toppings. In several recipes we simply crisp the tortilla under the broiler before adding different toppings. These versions are simple to fix and low in calories. In another recipe we brown the tortilla in bacon drippings for extra flavor.

Vegetarian Croissant

Storing unused avocado is easy. Leave the seed in and the peel on, wrap in plastic wrap, and refrigerate for up to 2 days.

1 croissant
  Dijon-style mustard
  Lettuce leaf
1 slice Swiss cheese, cut in
  half diagonally
2 thin tomato slices*
½ avocado, peeled and sliced
  (optional)
2 tablespoons alfalfa sprouts
4 thin slices zucchini *or*
  cucumber*
1 fresh mushroom, sliced*
2 tablespoons mayonnaise *or*
  salad dressing
1 teaspoon milk
½ teaspoon snipped fresh dillweed *or* basil, *or* dash
  dried dillweed *or* basil,
  crushed

● If desired, wrap croissant in foil and heat in a 350° oven about 4 minutes or just till warm. Split croissant, then spread lightly with mustard.

● Arrange lettuce leaf, Swiss cheese, tomato slices, avocado, sprouts, zucchini or cucumber, and mushroom slices on bottom half of croissant. Combine mayonnaise, milk, and dillweed or basil. Spoon over filling. Add top half of croissant. Makes 1 serving.

*You may substitute any of your favorite fresh vegetables for the tomato, zucchini, cucumber, or mushroom. Some vegetables, such as green beans, thinly sliced carrots, or asparagus, are especially good when steamed for a few minutes and then marinated for several hours in a vinaigrette dressing.

Shrimp in Croissant

Treat yourself to an elegant and delicious shrimp sandwich.

4 ounces fresh *or* frozen large
  shrimp in shells
1 tablespoon dry white wine
  or lemon juice
¼ teaspoon garlic powder
  Dash dried dillweed
2 tablespoons soft-style
  cream cheese
1 teaspoon chopped chives
1 croissant, split

● Thaw shrimp, if frozen. Shell and devein shrimp. Halve shrimp lengthwise. Combine wine, garlic powder, and dillweed. Dip shrimp in wine mixture, coating well, and place on an unheated rack of a small broiler pan. Broil 4 inches from the heat for 3 minutes. Turn; broil for 1 to 2 minutes more or till shrimp is opaque. Remove shrimp and keep warm.

● Meanwhile, combine cream cheese and chives. Spread cream cheese mixture on split croissant. Place on rack in broiler pan and broil 4 inches from the heat about 1 minute or till toasted. Remove from oven. Arrange shrimp on toasted croissant. Makes 1 serving.

Vegetarian Croissant

Sauced Tuna Pita

A low-in-calorie tuna pita with the fresh taste and crunch of a cucumber sauce.

Green Sauce
1 3¼-ounce can tuna *or*
    ½ of a 6½-ounce can tuna,
    drained and flaked
½ small carrot, finely
    shredded (2 tablespoons)
1 large pita round, split
    crosswise
   Lettuce leaves *or* alfalfa
    sprouts

● Prepare Green Sauce. In a small bowl combine tuna, carrot, and Green Sauce. Toss gently.

● At serving time, line each pita pocket with lettuce leaves or alfalfa sprouts. Spoon half of the tuna mixture into each pita pocket. Makes 1 serving.

Green Sauce: In a small bowl combine ¼ cup plain *yogurt;* ¼ large *cucumber,* peeled and chopped; 2 teaspoons minced *chives;* ½ teaspoon *lemon juice;* ¼ teaspoon dried *dillweed;* ⅛ teaspoon *salt;* and dash *paprika.* Mix well and chill till serving time. Makes ⅓ cup.

Sauces Make Sandwiches Special

Adding a bit of sauce, such as tasty Green Sauce (see recipe, above), will perk up any sandwich. Keep a few sauces in your refrigerator to spread on crisp tostadas, chewy pita rounds, or toasted English muffins. Then add your favorite meat or cheese and you are on your way to a great sandwich.

If you have cooked lamb or dark turkey meat, you can stuff a pita round with the thinly sliced meat, shredded lettuce, and a dollop of Green Sauce. As a versatile and easy sauce, prepare Tangy Blender Mayonnaise (see recipe, page 79). When you're ready to use it, just stir in the extra ingredients to make whichever sauce variation you choose.

Pastrami Sandwich Supreme

Most delicatessens will sell small amounts of coleslaw.

1	6-inch French-style roll
1	tablespoon mayonnaise *or* salad dressing
1	green onion, thinly sliced
½	teaspoon Dijon-style mustard
	Lettuce leaf
¼	cup coleslaw
	Tomato slices
½	of a 3-ounce package very thinly sliced pastrami
1	slice Swiss cheese

● Slice roll horizontally into 3 layers. Scoop out bottom roll slice, leaving a ¼-inch shell.

● Combine mayonnaise, green onion, and mustard. Mix well.

● To serve, spread bottom roll slice with *half* of the mayonnaise mixture. Top with a lettuce leaf. Spoon coleslaw onto lettuce-lined roll. Top with the tomato slices.

● Place middle slice of roll over tomato slices. Spread with remaining mayonnaise mixture. Arrange pastrami and Swiss cheese over mayonnaise. Top with remaining roll slice. Makes 1 sandwich.

Assembling the pastrami sandwich

A three-layer sandwich needs an anchor so the fillings will stay put and it will be easier to eat. After slicing the roll into three layers, scoop out the bottom layer, leaving a shell to "anchor" the fillings. Spread the shell with half of the mayonnaise mixture for flavor at the very bottom of the sandwich. Then tuck the lettuce leaf in the hollow to keep the coleslaw from soaking into the bread.

Pasta Salad Niçoise

This Mediterranean salad traditionally uses marinated cooked potatoes; our version uses marinated pasta shells for a new taste.

⅓ cup medium pasta shells *or*
    spirals (1 ounce)
¼ teaspoon dried dillweed
4 tablespoons Basic
    Vinaigrette (see recipe,
    page 78)
1 3¼-ounce can tuna *or* ½ of a
    6½-ounce can tuna,
    chilled
⅓ cup fresh *or* frozen cut
    green beans
    Lettuce leaves
    Radicchio leaves (optional)
4 pitted ripe olives (optional)
3 *or* 4 tomato slices
1 hard-cooked egg, quartered
    (optional)
    Thinly sliced green onion
    (optional)
    Anchovy fillet (optional)
    Garlic toast (optional)

● Cook pasta according to package directions; drain. Rinse with cold water and drain again. Stir dillweed into vinaigrette. Combine pasta and *2 tablespoons* of the vinaigrette; cover and chill several hours or overnight. Drain tuna. In a small bowl toss together tuna and *1 tablespoon* of the vinaigrette; cover and chill. Cook green beans till crisp-tender. Cover and chill.

● When ready to serve, arrange lettuce and radicchio leaves, if desired, on a plate. Arrange pasta, tuna, beans, olives, tomato slices, and egg on lettuce. Top salad with green onion and anchovy fillet, if desired. Drizzle with remaining vinaigrette. Serve with garlic toast, if desired. Makes 1 serving.

Baked Puffy Cheese Sandwich

Assemble this sandwich the night before, then cover and refrigerate. You'll need to allow about 5 minutes more baking time.

2 slices bread
    Dijon-style mustard
3 ounces bulk pork sausage,
    cooked, drained, and
    broken into small
    pieces
2 tablespoons shredded
    cheddar *or* Monterey Jack
    cheese
1 egg, beaten
½ cup light cream *or* milk
⅛ teaspoon seasoned salt
    Dash bottled hot pepper
    sauce

● Trim bread into rounds to fit a 10-ounce casserole. Lightly spread with mustard. Place slice, mustard side up, in the greased casserole. Top with sausage and cheese. Cover with remaining bread, mustard side down.

● Combine egg, cream or milk, seasoned salt, and hot pepper sauce. Pour over sandwich in casserole. Bake in a 325° oven about 30 minutes or till egg mixture is set and sandwich is light and puffy. Serve at once. Makes 1 serving.

Pasta Salad Niçoise

Marinated Beef Salad

Purchase just the amount of roast beef you need at your delicatessan.

4 ounces roast beef, sliced and
   cut into ½-inch strips
¼ cup sliced fresh mushrooms
1 small clove garlic, minced
   Basic Vinaigrette
   (see recipe, page 78)
   Lettuce leaves
4 radishes, sliced
4 cherry tomatoes, halved
½ cup broccoli flowerets
1 green onion, thinly sliced

● Combine beef and mushrooms in a small bowl or plastic bag. Add garlic to vinaigrette. Pour *half* of the vinaigrette over beef and mushrooms and toss till well coated. Cover and marinate at room temperature for 30 minutes or in the refrigerator for up to 24 hours.

● Arrange lettuce leaves on a plate. Top with beef and mushrooms, radishes, tomatoes, broccoli, and green onion. Drizzle remaining vinaigrette over vegetables. Makes 1 serving.

Gingered Chicken Salad

A tangy ginger dressing combines with chicken and fruit for a light dinner or luncheon salad.

1 tablespoon mayonnaise *or*
   salad dressing
1 tablespoon plain yogurt
½ teaspoon grated gingerroot
   or ⅛ teaspoon ground
   ginger
¼ teaspoon Dijon-style
   mustard
⅓ cup seedless red *or* green
   grapes, halved
⅓ cup chopped celery
1 tablespoon raisins
4 ounces cooked chicken, cut
   into bite-size strips (about
   ¾ cup)
   Lettuce leaves
1 teaspoon sunflower nuts
   Thin orange slice *or* wedge
   (optional)

● In a small bowl combine mayonnaise, yogurt, gingerroot, and mustard. Add grapes, celery, and raisins. Add chicken pieces; toss lightly to coat. Cover and chill for 30 minutes.

● Serve salad on lettuce leaves and sprinkle with sunflower nuts. Garnish with an orange slice or wedge, if desired. Makes 1 serving.

Zesty Baked Potato Skins

Next time, substitute 2 tablespoons finely chopped fully cooked ham for the bacon.

1 baking potato
2 tablespoons margarine *or* butter, softened
Dash salt
Dash pepper
1 tablespoon steak sauce *or* salsa
2 tablespoons dairy sour cream
2 slices bacon, crisp-cooked, drained, and crumbled
2 tablespoons sliced green onion
2 tablespoons chopped green pepper
⅓ cup shredded cheddar *or* Swiss cheese

● Scrub potato well; prick with a fork. Bake in a 425° oven about 40 minutes or till tender.

● Cool slightly. Cut lengthwise into quarters. Remove cooked potato insides, leaving ⅜-inch shells. (Reserve cooked potato for soup, potato salad, or another use.) Place shells, cut side up, in a baking pan. Brush with margarine or butter; sprinkle with salt and pepper.

● Broil 4 inches from the heat for 1 to 2 minutes or till crisp. Brush with steak sauce or salsa. Spoon sour cream on each shell and sprinkle with bacon, green onion, and green pepper. Top with shredded cheese. Return to broiler and broil about 1 minute or till cheese melts. Makes 1 serving.

Scooping out potato skins
Use a spoon to scoop out the slightly cooled baked potato, leaving ⅜-inch shells. Then, brush the skins with margarine or butter and broil them till they're crisp.

Chilled Chicken Soup

This elegant but easy chicken soup has just a hint of curry.

1 tablespoon finely chopped
   onion
1 tablespoon margarine *or*
   butter
1 tablespoon all-purpose flour
¼ to ½ teaspoon curry powder
½ teaspoon instant chicken
   bouillon granules
   Dash white pepper
½ cup water
½ cup light cream
½ cup finely diced cooked
   chicken
1 tablespoon vermouth
   Snipped fresh chives *or*
   toasted coconut (optional)

● In a small saucepan cook onion in margarine or butter till tender. Stir in flour, curry powder, bouillon granules, and pepper to blend. Add water all at once. Cook and stir till thickened and bubbly. Cook and stir for 1 minute more. Stir in cream, chicken pieces, and vermouth. Cover and chill for at least 2 hours. Garnish with fresh chives or toasted coconut, if desired. Makes 1 serving.

Turkey-Rice Soup

Marsala or sherry adds a special flavor to this nutritious and easy-to-make soup.

1¼ cups water
1 small onion, chopped
   (¼ cup)
1 small carrot, bias sliced
   (¼ cup)
1 tablespoon long grain rice
1 teaspoon instant chicken
   bouillon granules
⅛ teaspoon dried basil,
   crushed
½ cup diced cooked turkey *or*
   chicken
¼ cup frozen peas
1 tablespoon dry Marsala *or*
   dry sherry

● In a 1½-quart saucepan combine water, onion, carrot, *uncooked* rice, bouillon granules, and basil. Bring to boiling, then reduce heat. Cover and simmer mixture about 15 minutes or till rice is tender.

● Stir in turkey or chicken and peas; simmer, uncovered, about 5 minutes or till vegetables are tender. Stir in Marsala or sherry. Makes 1 serving.

Speedy Vegetable-Sausage Soup

A flavorful soup using fresh or frozen vegetables. When using leftover cooked vegetables, just reduce the simmering time.

1   6-ounce can vegetable juice cocktail
¼   cup water
1   small clove garlic, minced
¼   teaspoon Italian seasoning
    Dash pepper
¾   cup fresh *or* frozen mixed vegetables
3   ounces brown-and-serve sausage, sliced (3 to 4 links)
    Toast sticks *or* garlic bread (optional)

● In a medium saucepan combine vegetable juice, water, garlic, Italian seasoning, and pepper. Add vegetables. Bring to boiling; reduce heat. Cover and simmer till vegetables are tender, adding sausage links during the last 5 minutes of cooking. (Allow about 10 minutes for frozen vegetables and about 25 minutes for fresh vegetables.) Serve with toast sticks or garlic bread, if desired. Makes 1 serving.

Hearty Fish Stew

A fish stew that gives the versatility of using any kind of boneless fish fillet.

2   tablespoons chopped onion
1   small clove garlic, minced
1   teaspoon cooking oil
1   6-ounce can vegetable juice cocktail
¼   cup sliced carrot
¼   cup chopped fresh mushrooms
½   teaspoon instant chicken bouillon granules
¼   teaspoon dried basil, crushed
¼   teaspoon dried thyme, crushed
¼   teaspoon Worcestershire sauce
    Dash pepper
4   ounces fish fillet, cut into 1-inch pieces

● In a small saucepan cook onion and garlic in hot oil till onion is tender. Add juice, carrot, mushrooms, bouillon granules, basil, thyme, Worcestershire sauce, and pepper. Cover and simmer about 15 minutes or till vegetables are tender.

● Add fish pieces to saucepan. Cook for 2 to 3 minutes or till fish flakes easily with a fork. Makes 1 serving.

Tarragon Shrimp Salad

Tarragon Shrimp Salad

Cutting the shrimp in half gives more tarragon dressing flavor to each piece.

4 ounces medium-size shrimp, cleaned and cooked
3 tablespoons mayonnaise *or* salad dressing
1 green onion, thinly sliced
1 teaspoon lemon juice
½ teaspoon milk
⅛ to ¼ teaspoon dried tarragon, crushed
  Dash salt
  Dash lemon pepper
  Chopped lettuce
½ teaspoon capers (optional)
  Lemon wedges, dipped in paprika (optional)

● Cut shrimp in half lengthwise.

● In a small bowl combine mayonnaise, green onion, lemon juice, milk, tarragon, salt, and lemon pepper.

● Stir shrimp into mixture; cover and chill till serving time. Serve on lettuce. Sprinkle with capers and garnish with lemon wedges dipped in paprika, if desired. Makes 1 serving.

Salad Greens Can 'Make' A Salad

One serving of delicious salad on a pretty plate can be made elegant with some of the lovely salad greens on the market, such as escarole, curly endive, Oriental kale (used at left), mustard greens, or even crinkly leaf lettuce. To prepare salad greens, wash them in lots of cold water.

Place greens on paper towels or a clean kitchen towel and gently pat dry.

Reclosable plastic bags are great for storing salad greens in your refrigerator till you are ready to use them. When properly stored, greens may be kept for three or four days.

Quick Pizza Tostada

A great way to combine the flavors of pizza with a thin crispy tostada.

1 **6-inch flour tortilla**
2 **tablespoons tomato sauce**
     ***or* pizza sauce**
¼ **cup shredded herb-**
     flavored *or* mozzarella
     cheese (1 ounce)
1 **tablespoon cooked**
     pepperoni pieces *or*
     4 pepperoni slices,
     chopped
     Snipped fresh basil
     (optional)

● Place tortilla under the broiler. Broil 3 inches from the heat about 2 minutes or till crisp, turning once. Remove tortilla from broiler.

● Spread tortilla with tomato sauce or pizza sauce. Top with herb cheese and pepperoni. Return to broiler and broil for 1½ to 2 minutes or till cheese melts. Garnish with fresh basil, if desired. Makes 1 serving.

The toaster oven advantage
You'll find this appliance especially useful when cooking for one. Use it to toast, broil, brown, and bake without heating up your whole kitchen. Keep the instruction book handy and take advantage of the many features designed to make your cooking even more convenient.

Peanut Butter and Bacon Tostada

This is a quick and nutritious snack—you may want to add raisins or chopped apple.

1 6-inch flour tortilla
1 tablespoon chunk-style peanut butter
1 slice bacon, crisp-cooked, drained, and crumbled; *or* 1 tablespoon cooked bacon pieces

● Place tortilla under the broiler. Broil 3 inches from the heat about 2 minutes or till crisp, turning once. Remove tortilla from broiler.

● Spread tortilla with peanut butter. Top with bacon. Return to broiler and broil for 40 to 45 seconds more or till heated through. Makes 1 serving.

Bacon-Lettuce-Tomato Tostada

All the flavors of the popular BLT, plus a surprise dressing and cheese.

1 6-inch flour tortilla
2 slices bacon
1 tablespoon mayonnaise *or* salad dressing
1 tablespoon salsa
1 teaspoon milk
   Lettuce leaves
¼ cup shredded Swiss *or* Monterey Jack cheese (1 ounce)
½ small tomato, sliced

● Cut tortilla into quarters. In an 8-inch skillet cook bacon till crisp; drain and halve bacon, reserving 1 teaspoon of the drippings in skillet. Reheat skillet over medium heat. Add tortilla pieces to the skillet and cook for 3 to 4 minutes or till golden brown, turning to cook both sides. Remove from skillet.

● Combine mayonnaise, salsa, and milk. Top cooked tortilla quarters with a layer of lettuce, cheese, and tomato slices. Top with bacon pieces. Spoon mayonnaise mixture over bacon. Makes 1 serving.

Tostada Salad

All the flavors of Taco Salad, with a crispy flour tortilla that is broiled instead of deep-fried.

½ cup Basic Ground Beef
  Mixture (see recipe, below)
1 tablespoon salsa
1 6-inch flour tortilla
½ teaspoon margarine *or*
  butter, softened
1 tablespoon refried beans *or*
  bean dip
⅓ cup shredded cheddar
  cheese
  Torn lettuce
½ small tomato, sliced
½ avocado, seeded, peeled, and
  sliced crosswise
  Pitted ripe olives, sliced
  (optional)

● In a small saucepan heat meat mixture and salsa. Spread both sides of tortilla with margarine or butter. Place on an ungreased baking sheet and broil 3 inches from the heat for 2 to 3 minutes or till golden, turning once. Remove tortilla from broiler. Spread with refried beans or bean dip. Reserve *1 tablespoon* cheese for topping; sprinkle remaining cheese over tortilla. Return tortilla to broiler and broil for 30 seconds to 1 minute more or till cheese melts. Cut tortilla into quarters.

● For salad, arrange a layer of lettuce on a plate. Top with meat mixture and surround with tortilla quarters, tomato, and avocado. Sprinkle with reserved cheese and olives, if desired. Makes 1 serving.

Basic Ground Beef Mixture

This easy-to-make beef mixture can be an emergency shelf ingredient in your freezer.

1 pound lean ground beef
1 small onion, chopped
1 clove garlic, minced
1 teaspoon Worcestershire
  sauce
⅛ teaspoon salt
  Dash pepper

● In a large skillet cook meat, onion, and garlic till meat is brown and onion is tender; drain. Stir in Worcestershire sauce, salt, and pepper till well combined. Use 1 portion of the meat mixture right away and/or freeze portions for later use. Makes three ½-cup portions.

Note: To freeze, spoon ½-cup servings of meat mixture into freezer containers. Seal, label, and freeze. Thaw meat mixture at room temperature about 25 minutes or in the refrigerator overnight before using. One container of meat mixture is used in the Tostada Salad (see recipe, above), Easy Stroganoff Pasta Supper (see recipe, opposite), and Speedy Beef Casserole (see recipe, page 47).

Easy Stroganoff Pasta Supper

The pasta and meat cook together for a one-pot stroganoff.

1 ounce medium shell pasta (⅓ cup)
1 cup water
1 teaspoon margarine *or* butter
½ cup Basic Ground Beef Mixture (see recipe, opposite)
1 teaspoon instant beef bouillon granules
¼ teaspoon dried thyme, crushed
¼ cup milk
1 teaspoon all-purpose flour
3 fresh mushrooms, sliced
1 tablespoon dairy sour cream
1 teaspoon snipped parsley, chives, *or* green onion tops

● In a medium saucepan cook pasta in water and margarine or butter for 5 minutes, stirring occasionally. *Do not drain.* Add meat mixture, bouillon granules, and thyme. Bring to boiling; reduce heat. Simmer for 2 to 3 minutes or till pasta is tender and meat mixture is heated through.

● Meanwhile, combine milk and flour. Stir into the saucepan; add mushrooms. Cook and stir over medium heat till thickened and bubbly, then cook and stir for 1 minute more. Just before serving, stir in sour cream. Heat gently; *do not boil.* Top with snipped parsley, chives, or green onion tops. Makes 1 serving.

Linguine Primavera with Clams

This primavera combines pasta, clams, and broccoli in an easy one-dish meal.

1 ounce linguine
½ cup broccoli flowerets
1 tablespoon margarine *or* butter
⅓ cup milk
½ of a 6-ounce can clams (¼ cup liquid and 3 tablespoons clams)
2 teaspoons cornstarch
¼ teaspoon dried basil, crushed
Grated Parmesan cheese

● Cook linguine according to package directions, then drain. Keep warm. Meanwhile, in a medium skillet cook broccoli in margarine or butter over medium heat about 3 minutes or till crisp-tender.

● For sauce, stir together milk, clam liquid, and cornstarch; add clams and basil. Pour mixture into skillet. Cook and stir about 2 minutes or till thickened and bubbly. Add *cooked* linguine; cook and stir till heated through. Sprinkle with Parmesan cheese. Makes 1 serving.

Main Meals

If you have
a favorite cooking method and a favorite
fish, fowl, or meat, you'll find
them in this chapter. Here are baked,
broiled, simmered,
stir-fried, and microwave-cooked main
dishes to whet your appetite.

Trendy Food

Food trends today include new food products, new or newly discovered cooking techniques, and flavoring ingredients that are used by a large number of consumers.

A growing interest in pasta dishes is a general food trend. Fresh turkey parts in many forms are new products. The use of Oriental products such as oyster sauce and five-spice powder illustrates the interest of Americans in Oriental cookery. The increased use of herbs and wine rather than salt and salt-based products for flavoring is a health trend. You'll find recipes throughout this book that reflect these food trends, and the trend to healthier eating by using less fat, less salt, less sugar, more vegetables, and recommended amounts of protein.

Planning Oven Meals

Plan an oven meal for those times when you have lots to do. The food will cook in the oven while you go about your work or activity. Plan ahead and bake several foods at the same time—a main dish, a baked potato, rice for another meal, or a muffin for breakfast. Winter squash and apples can bake in the oven with your entrée. If cleanup time is at a premium, try one of the oven meals that bakes in a foil packet.

Stir-Frying

Stir-frying is an easy cooking method for a single-serving recipe. It's quick, needs no special equipment, and suits all levels of cooking skills. A nonstick skillet works just as well as a wok. Grocery stores sell vegetables in bulk, making it easy to buy just the right amount for one serving. If your grocery store sells carry-out salads, select cut-up vegetables from the salad bar.

Creamy Seafood in Toast Cup

Crab-flavored fish sticks are ideal for cooking for one; you can buy them individually in the deli. This recipe uses four.

Toast Cup (see recipe, page 47)
- 3 fresh mushrooms, sliced
- 1 tablespoon sliced green onion
- 1 tablespoon margarine *or* butter
- ½ cup milk *or* light cream
- 1½ teaspoons cornstarch
  Dash dried thyme, crushed
  Drop Worcestershire sauce
- 4 ounces frozen crab-flavored fish sticks, thawed and cut into 1-inch pieces
- 3 tablespoons dry white wine *or* dry sherry
  Dash salt
  Dash pepper
  Grated Parmesan cheese
  Cherry tomatoes, sliced (optional)
  Fresh dillweed (optional)

● Prepare Toast Cup. In a small saucepan cook mushrooms and green onion in margarine or butter till tender.

● Combine milk or cream, cornstarch, thyme, and Worcestershire sauce. Stir into mushroom mixture; cook and stir till thickened and bubbly. Carefully stir in fish pieces and wine. Heat gently for 1 minute. Season to taste with salt and pepper.

● Spoon into prepared Toast Cup. Sprinkle with Parmesan cheese. Garnish with cherry tomatoes and dillweed, if desired. Makes 1 serving.

Poached Salmon with Watercress Sauce

Poaching salmon is quick and easy. The Watercress Sauce adds flavor and color.

- 6 ounces fresh *or* frozen salmon steak, cut ¾ inch thick
  Watercress Sauce (see recipe, page 81)
- 1 cup water
- 2 teaspoons lemon juice
- 1 small bay leaf
- 2 whole peppercorns

● Thaw salmon steak, if frozen. Prepare Watercress Sauce; keep warm.

● In a medium skillet combine water, lemon juice, bay leaf, and peppercorns. Bring to boiling. Add salmon steak to the skillet. Reduce the heat and simmer, covered, for 6 to 8 minutes or till fish flakes easily when tested with a fork.

● Transfer fish to a plate. Spoon Watercress Sauce over fish. Makes 1 serving.

Creamy Seafood in Toast Cup

Glazed Ham Slice with Sweet Potatoes

Use the other half of the ham slice in an omelet, main dish salad, or one of the Breakfast-To-Go Sandwiches.

1 **8-ounce can sweet potatoes, drained**
2 **teaspoons margarine *or* butter, softened**
   Dash salt
   Dash pepper
1 **tablespoon pineapple preserves *or* apricot preserves**
¼ **teaspoon horseradish mustard**
½ **of an 8-ounce fully cooked ham slice**

● In a small bowl combine sweet potatoes, margarine or butter, salt, and pepper. Mix till well blended. Spoon into a greased 6-ounce custard cup. Bake in a 350° oven for 15 minutes.

● Meanwhile, combine pineapple or apricot preserves and horseradish mustard. Place ham slice in a 10x6x2-inch baking dish. Spread with preserves mixture. Place in 350° oven with sweet potatoes; bake about 10 minutes or till both ham and potatoes are heated through. Makes 1 serving.

Baked Pork Chop with Squash

The unusual flavor combination of brown sugar, thyme, and lemon peel bakes atop the yellow squash. Yummy with a baked pork chop.

1 **6-ounce pork loin rib chop, cut ½ inch thick**
1 **teaspoon milk**
   Dash salt
   Dash pepper
1 **tablespoon fine dry bread crumbs**
1 **tablespoon finely chopped almonds**
2 **teaspoons margarine *or* butter, melted**
   Dash paprika
1 **small yellow summer squash, halved lengthwise and cut into ¼-inch slices (¾ cup)**
1 **teaspoon brown sugar**
¼ **teaspoon dried thyme, crushed**
¼ **teaspoon finely shredded lemon peel**

● Trim excess fat from chop. Brush chop with milk. Sprinkle lightly with salt and pepper.

● In a small bowl combine bread crumbs, almonds, *1 teaspoon* of the melted margarine or butter, and paprika. Place chops in a shallow baking dish. Top with almond mixture. Bake, covered, in a 375° oven for 30 minutes. Uncover and bake for 10 to 15 minutes more or till tender.

● Meanwhile, place squash in an 8- or 10-ounce baking dish. Top with brown sugar, thyme, and lemon peel. Drizzle with remaining melted margarine. Place in the 375° oven with the chop. Bake, covered, for 10 minutes. Stir well; cover and bake for 5 to 10 minutes or till tender. Makes 1 serving.

Speedy Beef Casserole

Make your freezer an emergency shelf. Then thaw Basic Ground Beef Mixture, Fresh Tomato Sauce, and cooked rice in your refrigerator during the day for an easy supper.

½ cup Basic Ground Beef
    Mixture (see recipe,
    page 40)
½ cup Fresh Tomato Sauce*
    (see recipe, page 78)
½ cup cooked rice
¼ teaspoon chili powder
¼ cup shredded cheddar
    cheese (1 ounce)

● In a small saucepan combine meat mixture, tomato sauce, rice, and chili powder. Cook over medium-high heat about 10 minutes or till hot and bubbly, stirring occasionally. Stir in *half* of the cheese till melted.

● Spoon onto a plate. Top with remaining shredded cheese. Makes 1 serving.

*You may substitute canned Italian-style tomato sauce for the Fresh Tomato Sauce.

How to make a Toast Cup
Lightly butter both sides of a slice of bread. Gently press into a 6-ounce custard cup, shaping bread into a basket. Bake in a 375° oven for 15 to 20 minutes or till golden brown.

    You may prefer to make several cups at one time. After baking, let them cool. Then wrap them individually in moisture- and vaporproof material and freeze.

Florentine Lasagna Rosettes

Ground pork or ground beef work well in place of the turkey in this versatile dish. (Also pictured on the cover and page 50.)

½ of a 10-ounce package
   frozen chopped spinach,
   thawed and drained
   (½ cup)
1 lasagna noodle (1 ounce)
1 single-serving envelope
   instant cream of chicken
   soup mix
½ cup hot water
¼ cup shredded Swiss *or*
   Colby cheese
4 ounces ground raw turkey
1 tablespoon chopped onion
¼ teaspoon dried thyme,
   crushed

● Squeeze excess liquid from spinach; set aside. Cook lasagna noodle according to package directions; drain. In a small saucepan combine soup mix, water, and cheese. Heat over medium heat till well blended and cheese is melted; remove from heat.

● In a medium skillet cook ground turkey and onion till meat is no longer pink and onion is tender. Drain. Stir in spinach, thyme, and *half* of the cheese mixture. Mix well.

● Meanwhile, halve lasagna noodle lengthwise. In a small greased baking dish curl each half into a rosette about 2½ inches in diameter. Spoon turkey mixture into the lasagna rosettes (see photo, page 50). Spoon remaining cheese mixture over rosettes. Bake, covered, in a 350° oven for 25 to 30 minutes or till heated through. To serve, spoon extra sauce from dish over rosettes. Makes 1 serving.

Rigatoni with Sausage

A Cooking for One *version of Pasta with Carbonara Sauce.*

1 egg
2 tablespoons milk
1 tablespoon grated
   Parmesan cheese
⅛ teaspoon salt
   Dash pepper
¾ cup rigatoni (2 ounces)
6 ounces bulk Italian sausage
1 teaspoon snipped parsley
   Grated Parmesan cheese

● In a small mixing bowl combine egg, milk, 1 tablespoon cheese, salt, and pepper till just combined.

● Cook rigatoni according to package directions; drain. In a skillet cook sausage till brown. Break into small pieces.

● Add cooked rigatoni to skillet and toss with sausage till warm. Remove skillet from heat. Pour egg mixture into the skillet, and toss till pasta is well coated. Sprinkle with parsley and additional cheese. Serve immediately. Makes 1 serving.

Florentine Lasagna Rosettes

Skillet Veal Parmesan

3 tablespoons grated
   Parmesan cheese
1 tablespoon fine dry
   bread crumbs
   Dash garlic powder
   Dash pepper
4 ounces veal cutlet,
   cut ¼ inch thick
2 tablespoons milk
1 tablespoon cooking oil
1 8-ounce can tomato sauce
1 tablespoon dry white
   wine
¼ teaspoon Italian
   seasoning
½ cup coarsely chopped
   zucchini
   Hot cooked noodles

● Combine *1 tablespoon* Parmesan cheese, crumbs, garlic powder, and pepper. Dip veal in milk; coat with crumb mixture.

● In an 8-inch skillet cook veal in hot oil over medium-low heat about 8 minutes or just till tender, turning once. In a small bowl mix tomato sauce, wine, and Italian seasoning; add to skillet.

● Cook and stir over medium heat till thickened. Add zucchini. Cover and simmer about 5 minutes or till zucchini is crisp-tender. Sprinkle with *2 tablespoons* cheese. Serve over hot cooked noodles. Makes 1 serving.

Shaping and filling the Florentine Lasagna Rosettes
Cook and cool a lasagna noodle; cut the noodle in half lengthwise. In the baking dish, place noodle cut-side down and wrap it around in spiral fashion to make a 2½-inch rosette, leaving space for filling. Spoon the filling into the rosette shape (see recipe, page 48).

This dish looks elegant and complicated, but it is actually easy to make and fun to eat.

50

Quick One-Pot Spaghetti and Meatballs

Pasta cooks in the spaghetti sauce, then ground beef is dropped by spoonfuls into the sauce mixture. How easy!

⅔ cup spaghetti sauce
⅔ cup water
1 ounce spaghetti, broken
   (¼ cup)
4 ounces ground beef round,
   or ground raw turkey
3 medium mushrooms, sliced
2 green onions, sliced
4 pimiento-stuffed olives
   or pitted ripe olives,
   sliced
Grated Parmesan cheese
Garlic toast (optional)

● In a medium saucepan combine spaghetti sauce and water; bring to boiling. Add pasta and cook, covered, for 5 minutes.

● Drop meat by small spoonfuls into sauce mixture. Add mushrooms and green onions. Return to boiling; reduce heat.

● Cover and simmer about 10 minutes or till meatballs and pasta are done and vegetables are tender, stirring twice. Stir in olives and heat through.

● Sprinkle with Parmesan cheese; serve with garlic toast, if desired. Makes 1 serving.

Making easy "meatballs"
Spaghetti sauce, pasta, and meatballs all cook in the same pot—just use a spoon to scoop up the lean ground beef and drop it into hot sauce mixture. Lean ground beef is best to use because it contains the least fat.

If you have any extra spaghetti and meatballs, try using them in a sandwich.

Pepper-Beef Stir-Fry

Pepper-Beef Stir-Fry

Most grocery stores have vegetables available in bulk so you can buy just three mushrooms and three cherry tomatoes for stir-frying.

4 ounces beef top round steak
1 tablespoon soy sauce
1 tablespoon water
1 small clove garlic, minced
  Dash pepper
1 teaspoon cornstarch
1 tablespoon cooking oil
¼ green pepper, cut into ¾-inch pieces
2 green onions, bias-sliced into 1-inch lengths (¼ cup)
3 fresh medium mushrooms, sliced
3 cherry tomatoes, halved
  Hot cooked noodles (optional)

● Partially freeze beef; cut on the bias into thin slices. For marinade, stir together soy sauce, water, garlic, and pepper. Add beef, stirring to coat well. Cover and marinate at room temperature for 30 minutes or in the refrigerator for 2 hours, stirring occasionally. Drain beef, reserving marinade. Add enough water to reserved marinade to make ⅓ cup. Stir in cornstarch. Set cornstarch mixture aside.

● Preheat a medium skillet over high heat; add oil. Add pepper pieces, green onion, and mushrooms; stir-fry about 2 minutes or till vegetables are crisp-tender. Remove vegetables from skillet. (Add more oil as necessary during cooking.)

● Add beef to the skillet. Stir-fry for 2 to 3 minutes or till done. Push mixture from center of the skillet.

● Stir cornstarch mixture; add to center of the skillet. Cook and stir till thickened and bubbly. Cook and stir for 30 seconds more. Return vegetables; stir ingredients together. Stir in tomatoes. Cook and stir for 1 minute more. Serve over hot cooked noodles, if desired. Makes 1 serving.

Chicken Livers in Wine Stir-Fry

No red wine on hand? White wine will also flavor these chicken livers perfectly.

¼ cup water
¼ cup dry red wine *or* chicken broth
1 teaspoon cornstarch
1 slice bacon, cut up
2 green onions, thinly sliced (¼ cup)
3 fresh mushrooms, sliced
4 ounces chicken livers
  Dash salt
  Dash pepper
  Toast points *or* hot cooked rice
  Tomato wedges (optional)

● For sauce, stir together water, wine or broth, and cornstarch. Set aside. In a medium skillet cook bacon till crisp. Add green onions and mushrooms. Stir-fry for 1 to 2 minutes or till crisp-tender; push to one side. Add chicken livers. Stir-fry over medium heat for 5 to 7 minutes or till livers are no longer pink. Push chicken livers from center of skillet.

● Stir sauce; add to center of skillet. Cook and stir till thickened and bubbly. Cook and stir for 1 minute more. Gently stir ingredients together to coat with sauce. Season to taste with salt and pepper. Serve with toast points or over rice. Garnish with tomato wedges, if desired. Makes 1 serving.

Meals As Easy As 1-2-3

Meals as easy as 1-2-3 simply means buying or cooking a larger amount of a staple ingredient, such as rice or potatoes, and planning for its use in several different meals rather than just one. The same planning works for buying or cooking fish, meats, poultry, pasta (see information at right), or fruits and vegetables. Here are a few examples.

RICE

Prepare according to package directions, making enough to yield several portions.

1. Use one portion of hot cooked *rice* as a side dish with poultry, fish, or meat.

2. Heat one portion of cooked *rice* to use as a base for creamed vegetables or seafood. Or, use it in Creamy Seafood in Toast Cup instead of the toast cup (see recipe, page 44).

3. Use one portion of cooked *rice* for dessert: Combine cooked rice with fruit, vanilla yogurt, and a little whipped cream.

POTATOES

Cook several medium potatoes.

1. Use one hot cooked *potato,* buttered or mashed, as a side dish with a meal.

2. Slice one cooked *potato* for fried potatoes or for use in Vegetable Frittata (see recipe, page 15). Or, use it in Pasta Salad Niçoise instead of the pasta (see recipe, page 30).

3. Use one cooked *potato* in Dilled Potato Soup (see recipe, page 80). Or, make a quick potato salad: Combine cubed cooked potato with a little mayonnaise and cooked vegetables.

CHICKEN

Purchase a whole chicken (refrigerate or freeze portions to use as needed).

1. Use *chicken drumsticks and thighs* for Oriental Barbecued Chicken (see recipe, page 62).

2. Use *chicken breast halves* for Chicken Divan Stir-Fry (see recipe, page 61). Or, use them for an Italian Stuffed Chicken Breast (see recipe, page 72).

3. Cook portions of *chicken* and substitute chicken for turkey in Turkey-Rice Soup (see recipe, page 34). Or, use it in Gingered Chicken Salad (see recipe, page 32).

Hints for Using Pasta

Pasta, in a variety of sizes and shapes, is one of the most versatile staples you can have on hand. Use it for hot or cold salads, casseroles, pasta main dishes, soups, and side dishes. In fact, you can even decorate your kitchen with it. Store your favorite pastas in airtight jars and glass canisters.

Pasta comes in hundreds of shapes (five are shown at right), and if you look in your grocery store or specialty shop, you'll see variations in color, as well. Look for colorful vegetable pastas, tasty whole wheat pastas,

PASTA RECIPES
Here are some recipe examples where pasta is served hot or cold.

Use pasta hot:
Florentine Lasagna Rosettes *or* Rigatoni with Sausage (see recipes, page 48). Linguine Primavera with Clams (see recipe, page 41). Pasta and sauce cook at the same time in Easy Stroganoff Pasta Supper and Quick One-Pot Spaghetti and Meatballs (see recipes, pages 41 and 51).

Use pasta cold:
Pasta Salad Niçoise (see recipe, page 30).

and extra-nutritious lupini and triticale pastas.

Buying and storing pasta:
When stores sell bulk pasta, you can buy small quantities. If you purchase standard packages, be sure to store pasta in tightly covered containers in a cool, dry place. Dry pasta will keep for up to 2 years.

You should store fresh pasta in the refrigerator and use according to package directions.

Store cooked pasta in cold water in the refrigerator. When you're ready to use it, place the pasta in a strainer in a pan of boiling water and reheat for a few minutes.

Cooking pasta:
The Italians use the phrase *al dente* to describe pasta cooked to the just barely done stage. Follow package directions and cook pasta to suit your taste.

Keep a kitchen scale handy. The recipes in this book are planned for 1 or 2 ounces of pasta. If you don't have a scale, ⅓ cup of small or medium pasta equals about 1 ounce. For long pieces such as spaghetti, linguine, or vermicelli, a bunch about the diameter of a dime will be approximately 1 serving. Or divide an 8-ounce package into 8 portions.

Rigatoni (ridged tube)

Tortellini (small filled twists)

Conchiglie (medium shells)

Orzo (barley-shaped)

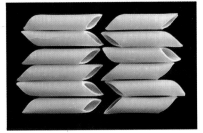
Mostaccioli or Penne (feathers or quills)

Scallop Stir-Fry

Be sure to wash scallops thoroughly to eliminate the sand trapped inside the shellfish.

4 ounces fresh *or* frozen scallops
¼ cup light cream
1 teaspoon all-purpose flour
1 teaspoon Dijon-style mustard
1 tablespoon cooking oil
3 fresh mushrooms, sliced
½ green onion, sliced
1 teaspoon lemon juice
Seashell-shaped puff pastry (see directions, page 58)

● Thaw scallops, if frozen. Cut any large scallops in half. For sauce, stir together cream, flour, and mustard. Set aside.

● Preheat a medium skillet over medium-high heat; add oil. (Add more oil as necessary during cooking.) Stir-fry mushrooms and green onion about 1 minute or till crisp-tender. Remove vegetables from skillet.

● Add scallops to the hot skillet. Stir-fry scallops about 2 minutes or till opaque. Remove scallops. Stir sauce; add to the skillet. Cook and stir till thickened and bubbly. Return vegetables and scallops to skillet. Add lemon juice. Cook and stir for 1 minute more. Serve over puff pastry. Makes 1 serving.

Far Eastern Rice Loaf

Try this unusual rice dish that's flavored with spices, nuts, garlic, and cooked fish. It's a version of the dish from India called kedgeree (KEDGE-ah-ree).

½ cup chopped celery
2 tablespoons chopped onion
1 small clove garlic, minced
1 tablespoon margarine *or* butter
¼ cup chopped nuts
¼ teaspoon ground turmeric
⅛ teaspoon ground cumin
Dash salt
Dash pepper
4 ounces cooked fish, flaked
½ cup cooked rice
1 cup chopped lettuce
Fresh cilantro *or* parsley (optional)
Pine nuts *or* slivered almonds (optional)

● In a small skillet cook celery, onion, and garlic in margarine or butter till onion is tender. Stir in chopped nuts, turmeric, cumin, salt, and pepper. Stir in fish and rice. Spoon into a lightly greased 15-ounce custard cup; press gently.

● Bake, uncovered, in a 350° oven about 20 minutes or till heated through. Arrange chopped lettuce on a plate. Invert fish loaf onto lettuce. Garnish with fresh cilantro and pine nuts, if desired. Makes 1 serving.

Scallop Stir-Fry

Here's how to make the shaped pastry that dresses up Scallop Stir-Fry (see recipe, page 56).

1 Cutting the puff pastry dough

Cut a 6x6-inch shell pattern from cardboard, using photo as a guide. (You can use the pastry package.) Place on top of unfolded partially thawed puff pastry dough. With a sharp knife, cut out the shell form by following the edge of the cardboard pattern.

Place the cutout pastry on an ungreased baking sheet. Score four grooves, ⅛ inch deep, from top to bottom as shown in photo. Don't slice through the pastry.

2 Baking the pastry shell

Brush the pastry with a little milk. Bake in a 375° oven for 20 to 25 minutes or till golden brown. Use as a base for Scallop Stir-Fry.

You may bake more than one shell at a time, then freeze the extra shells individually. To use, place frozen shell on an ungreased baking sheet. Bake in a 350° oven for 5 to 7 minutes or till shell is warm.

Spanish-Style Fish Fillet

Fish bakes in an easy sauce of tomato and green pepper.

4 ounces fresh *or* frozen
    fish fillet (about ½ inch
    thick)
Dash salt
Dash pepper
Dash paprika
2 tablespoons finely
    chopped green pepper
½ cup Fresh Tomato Sauce*
    (see recipe, page 78)
Hot cooked rice
2 pimiento-stuffed olives,
    sliced (optional)
Lemon wedges (optional)

● Thaw fish, if frozen. Place a 12x12-inch piece of heavy foil, dull-side down, in a pie plate, Place fish in center of foil. Sprinkle both sides of fish with salt, pepper, and paprika. Top with green pepper. Spoon tomato sauce over fish. Carefully fold two opposite sides of foil together; fold up remaining sides to seal.

● Bake in a 400° oven for 15 to 20 minutes or till fish flakes easily when tested with a fork. Place hot cooked rice on a plate; spoon fish and sauce over rice. If desired, top with sliced olives and garnish with lemon wedges. Makes 1 serving.

*You may substitute canned Italian-style tomato sauce for the Fresh Tomato Sauce.

Pork and Shrimp Stir-Fry

2 tablespoons plum wine
    or dry sherry
2 tablespoons soy sauce
    or teriyaki sauce
1 teaspoon sugar
1 teaspoon grated gingerroot
3 ounces boneless pork,
    bias sliced into thin
    strips
2 ounces frozen cooked
    shrimp, thawed
1 teaspoon cornstarch
1 tablespoon cooking oil
¼ cup slivered *or* sliced
    almonds
1 cup fresh bean sprouts
¼ cup chopped green pepper
2 green onions, thinly
    sliced (¼ cup)
1 clove garlic, minced
½ cup fresh *or* canned
    pineapple pieces

● For marinade, combine wine, soy sauce or teriyaki sauce, sugar, and gingerroot; add pork and shrimp. Let stand at room temperature for 15 minutes. Drain pork and shrimp, reserving the marinade. Combine reserved marinade and cornstarch. Set cornstarch mixture aside.

● Preheat a medium skillet over high heat; add cooking oil. (Add more oil as necessary during cooking.) Stir-fry almonds in hot oil about 30 seconds or till toasted. Add bean sprouts and stir-fry about 1 minute or till sprouts are crisp-tender. Transfer sprout mixture to a plate; keep warm.

● Add green pepper, onions, and garlic to skillet. Stir-fry about 1 minute or till crisp-tender. Remove vegetables from skillet. Add pork and shrimp to the hot skillet. Stir-fry about 3 minutes or till pork is no longer pink. Push pork and shrimp to one side.

● Stir cornstarch mixture; add to center of skillet. Cook and stir till thickened and bubbly. Cook and stir for 1 minute more; return vegetables. Add pineapple pieces to skillet; stir ingredients together till coated. Cook and stir for 1 minute more. Spoon over sprout mixture on plate. Makes 1 serving.

Chicken Divan Stir-Fry

Chicken Divan Stir-Fry

A new twist to the popular baked Chicken Divan.

6 ounces boneless chicken
   breast, skinned
3 tablespoons water *or* dry
   white wine
1 tablespoon lemon juice
1 teaspoon sugar
1 small clove garlic, minced
⅛ teaspoon curry powder
   Dash pepper
½ teaspoon cornstarch
1 tablespoon cooking oil
1 cup broccoli flowerets
2 green onions, cut into
   ½-inch pieces
1 tablespoon mayonnaise *or*
   salad dressing
   Hot cooked rice with dash of
   ground turmeric
   (optional)

● Cut chicken into thin strips. For marinade, combine water or wine, lemon juice, sugar, garlic, curry powder, and pepper. Add chicken, stirring to coat well. Let stand at room temperature for 20 to 30 minutes. Drain chicken, reserving marinade. If necessary, add enough water to reserved marinade to make ¼ cup liquid. Stir in cornstarch; set aside.

● Preheat a medium skillet over high heat; add cooking oil. (Add more oil as necessary during cooking.) Stir-fry broccoli and green onions in hot oil about 1½ minutes or till crisp-tender. Remove vegetables from skillet.

● Add chicken to hot skillet. Stir-fry about 2 minutes or till tender. Push chicken from center of skillet. Return vegetables; stir in cornstarch mixture. Cook about 1 minute more or till heated through. Remove from heat; stir in mayonnaise. Serve over hot cooked rice. Makes 1 serving.

Mexican Chicken Salad

All the flavor of a chicken taco in an easy main-dish salad for one.

6 ounces boneless chicken
   breast, cut into 1-inch
   pieces
1 teaspoon cooking oil
1 green onion, bias-sliced into
   ½-inch lengths
½ cup taco sauce
⅓ cup bean dip
   Chopped lettuce
½ cup shredded cheddar
   cheese (2 ounces)
   Tomato wedges
   Tortilla chips

● In a medium skillet cook and stir chicken pieces in hot oil over high heat about 3 minutes or till tender. Remove chicken pieces from skillet. (Add more oil as necessary during cooking.)

● Add green onion to skillet. Cook and stir about 1½ minutes or till crisp-tender. Return chicken to skillet; stir in taco sauce and bean dip. Cook and stir till heated through.

● Arrange lettuce on a plate; spoon chicken mixture over lettuce. Top with cheese; garnish with tomato wedges and tortilla chips. Makes 1 serving.

Oriental Barbecued Chicken

If chicken pieces are large, use any remaining cooked chicken in a sandwich, soup, or salad.

2 chicken drumsticks *or* thighs *or* ½ of a whole medium chicken breast
2 tablespoons frozen orange juice concentrate, thawed
2 tablespoons honey
1 tablespoon dried minced onion
1 tablespoon soy sauce
1 tablespoon prepared mustard
½ teaspoon grated gingerroot
Baked Rice with Fruit and Nuts (see recipe, page 82) (optional)

● Place chicken pieces in a heavy plastic bag; set in a shallow dish. For marinade, in a small bowl combine orange juice concentrate, honey, onion, soy sauce, mustard, and gingerroot. Pour over chicken in bag; close bag. Refrigerate for 2 to 18 hours, occasionally turning bag to coat chicken evenly with marinade.

● Assemble Baked Rice with Fruit and Nuts to bake with the chicken, if desired. Remove chicken pieces from bag, reserving the marinade. Place chicken pieces, skin side up, on a rack in a shallow baking pan.

● Bake chicken and rice together in a 350° oven for 35 to 40 minutes or till chicken and rice are tender. Turn chicken; brush with reserved marinade during last few minutes of baking time. Makes 1 serving.

Three-Way Kabobs

You get a choice of three different dinner kabobs with a variety of vegetables.

1 tablespoon lemon juice
1 tablespoon soy sauce
1 tablespoon hoisin sauce
1 tablespoon dry sherry *or* fruit juice
1 small clove garlic, minced
1 teaspoon sugar
4 ounces boneless chicken breast, beef, *or* lamb, cut in 1-inch pieces
½ medium zucchini, cut into ½-inch slices (⅔ cup)
½ medium red, green, *or* yellow sweet pepper, cut into 1-inch pieces (½ cup)
4 cherry tomatoes

● For marinade, in a small bowl combine lemon juice, soy sauce, hoisin sauce, sherry, garlic, and sugar. Stir chicken or meat pieces into marinade. Cover and marinate at room temperature for 30 minutes or in the refrigerator for 2 to 6 hours. Drain chicken or meat, reserving the marinade.

● Using two 6- or 8-inch skewers, alternately thread skewers with chicken or meat pieces, zucchini, and sweet pepper. Place kabobs on the unheated rack of a small broiler pan. Broil kabobs 4 inches from heat for 4 minutes for chicken or 6 minutes for beef or lamb.

● Brush reserved marinade on kabobs. Turn kabobs over and brush again with marinade. Broil for 4 to 5 minutes longer for chicken or 6 to 7 minutes for beef or lamb or till done, adding cherry tomatoes to the ends of skewers during the last 1 minute of broiling. Make 1 serving.

Tenderloin Deluxe with Parmesan Potatoes

Broiled tenderloin steak is a treat—especially with this brandy mushroom sauce.

1 small baking potato
3 teaspoons margarine *or*
    butter, melted
  Dash garlic salt
  Grated Parmesan cheese
4 ounces beef tenderloin,
    cut ¾ inch thick
3 fresh mushrooms, sliced
2 tablespoons brandy
1 small clove garlic, minced
  Dash pepper

● Cut potato in half lengthwise. Cut each half into 3 wedges. Place potato wedges on the unheated rack of a small broiler pan. Brush with *1 teaspoon* of the melted margarine or butter. Broil 4 inches from heat for 6 to 8 minutes or till almost brown. Turn; brush wedges with another *1 teaspoon* margarine. Sprinkle with garlic salt. Continue broiling for 4 minutes; sprinkle with Parmesan cheese. Broil for 2 to 4 minutes more or till brown. Remove and keep warm.

● Place tenderloin on broiler pan. Broil meat for 4 minutes. Turn; broil till meat is of desired doneness (allow 4 to 6 minutes more for medium-rare).

● In a small saucepan combine mushrooms, brandy, garlic, pepper, and remaining melted margarine. Cook over medium heat about 4 minutes or till mushrooms are tender. To serve, arrange tenderloin and potato wedges on a plate and spoon mushroom sauce over meat. Makes 1 serving.

Citrus Orange Roughy

Orange roughy is a New Zealand fish new to markets in the United States. It has a firm texture and a wonderfully mild flavor.

6	ounces fresh *or* frozen orange roughy fillet
¼	teaspoon finely shredded orange peel
¼	cup orange juice
1	tablespoon water
1	tablespoon lemon juice
1	tablespoon margarine *or* butter, melted
½	teaspoon sugar
⅛	teaspoon ground ginger
	Dash salt
½	teaspoon cornstarch
6	to 8 fresh pea pods (optional)
	Hot cooked rice (optional)
	Citrus curls
	Sliced almonds

● Thaw fish, if frozen. In a small bowl combine orange peel, orange juice, water, lemon juice, margarine or butter, sugar, ginger, and salt.

● Place fish on the unheated, lightly greased rack of a small broiler pan. Brush fish with some of the orange mixture. Broil fish 4 inches from heat till fish flakes easily when tested with a fork. (Allow 5 minutes for each ½ inch of thickness.) Remove from the oven; keep warm.

● Meanwhile, in a small saucepan combine remaining orange mixture and cornstarch. Cook and stir till thickened and bubbly; cook and stir for 2 minutes more.

● If using pea pods, steam them over boiling water about 4 minutes or till crisp-tender. To serve, arrange fish, pea pods, and rice on a plate. Spoon over orange sauce. Garnish with citrus curls and sliced almonds. Makes 1 serving.

Bacon Burger

Bacon, blue cheese, and steak sauce combine to give this burger an elegant taste.

4	ounces lean ground beef
2	slices bacon, crisp-cooked, drained, and crumbled
1	tablespoon crumbled blue cheese
½	teaspoon steak sauce
	Dash pepper
1	hamburger bun, split and toasted
	Tomato slice
	Lettuce leaf

● In a small bowl combine ground beef, bacon pieces, blue cheese, steak sauce, and pepper. Shape into a ½-inch-thick patty.

● Place patty on the unheated rack of a small broiler pan. Broil 3 to 4 inches from the heat till of desired doneness, turning once (allow about 12 minutes total time for medium). Serve on hamburger bun with tomato and lettuce. For an easy meal, add a salad from the delicatessen. Makes 1 serving.

Citrus Orange Roughy

Buttery Microwave Fish

4 ounces fresh *or* frozen
  fish fillet (½ inch thick)
Dash salt
Dash pepper
2 teaspoons butter *or*
  margarine
1 teaspoon lemon juice
Drop bottled hot pepper
  sauce
Dash paprika

● Thaw fish, if frozen. Place fish in a 10-ounce nonmetal oval baking dish. Sprinkle with salt and pepper. Cover with vented clear plastic wrap. Micro-cook on 100% power (high) about 2 minutes or till fish flakes easily when tested with a fork. Let the fish stand, covered, while preparing butter sauce.

● For butter sauce, in a 1-cup nonmetal measure or a 6-ounce custard cup, cook butter or margarine, lemon juice, and hot pepper sauce, uncovered, on high for 30 to 45 seconds or till butter is melted. Mix well. Transfer fish to a plate; drizzle with butter sauce. Sprinkle with paprika. Makes 1 serving.

Caper Microwave Fish: Prepare Buttery Microwave Fish as directed above, *except* add 1 teaspoon drained *capers* to butter sauce before cooking.

Oscar Microwave Fish: Prepare Buttery Microwave Fish as directed above, *except* add one 1-ounce frozen *crab-flavored fish stick,* thawed and chopped, *or* ¼ cup flaked canned *crabmeat* to butter sauce before cooking. To serve, arrange 2 cooked *asparagus spears* over fish, then top with sauce.

Dill Microwave Fish: Prepare the Buttery Microwave Fish as directed above, *except* add ⅛ teaspoon dried *dillweed* to butter sauce before cooking.

Parsley Microwave Fish: Prepare Buttery Microwave Fish as directed above, *except* add ½ teaspoon snipped *parsley* and ½ teaspoon *horseradish mustard* to butter sauce before cooking.

Testing the fish
For doneness

When you think the fish is almost done, insert the tines of a fork into the thickest part of the fish and twist the fork gently. The fish is done when it flakes easily and separates readily from any bones. Fish will have an opaque appearance and the juices will be milky white.

Micro-Cooking

Fish

Fish fillets such as halibut, haddock, and flounder can be cooked using these directions. If fillet varies in thickness, turn under any thin portion to obtain even thickness. Place fish in a nonmetal baking dish. Cover and micro-cook on 100% power (high) using these timings.

Fish (4 ounces)	Thickness	Time
Fresh fillet *or* frozen individual fillet, thawed	½ inch	2 minutes
Cut from block of frozen fish, thawed	1 inch	2½ to 3½ minutes

Roast Cornish Hen with Savory Fruit Stuffing

Try this recipe when you're really hungry. It makes a generous serving.

1   1½-pound fresh *or* frozen
    Cornish game hen
¼   cup water
2   tablespoons margarine *or*
    butter
1   cup onion-flavored
    croutons
2   tablespoons dried fruit
    bits
1   tablespoon finely
    chopped green onion
½   teaspoon instant chicken
    bouillon granules
1   tablespoon mayonnaise *or*
    salad dressing
⅛   teaspoon poultry
    seasoning
    Quick Cranberry Sauce
    for One (optional)

● Thaw hen, if frozen. Rinse hen with cold water and pat dry. For stuffing, in a small saucepan combine water and margarine or butter; cook till margarine melts. Remove from heat. Stir in croutons, fruit bits, onion, and bouillon granules.

● Spoon stuffing into body cavity. Combine mayonnaise and poultry seasoning; coat hen with mayonnaise mixture.

● Place hen, breast side up on a rack in a small shallow roasting pan. Roast, uncovered, in a 375° oven for 1 to 1¼ hours or till drumstick moves easily in socket. Serve with cranberry sauce, if desired. Makes 1 serving.

Quick Cranberry Sauce for One: In a small saucepan combine ½ cup fresh *or* frozen *cranberries,* 2 tablespoons *brown sugar,* and 1 tablespoon frozen *orange juice concentrate,* thawed. Bring to boiling. Reduce heat and simmer, uncovered, for 3 to 5 minutes or till cranberry skins pop. Cool. Makes ⅓ cup.

Carving a Cornish Game Hen

Remove stuffing from body cavity. Using a long sharp knife, split the roasted hen straight along center of the breast bone, making right and left halves of the cornish hen. If desired, use a small sharp flexible knife to cut off the legs and wings. Then slice the meat on the breast halves.

Roast Cornish Hen with
Savory Fruit Stuffing

Five-Spice-Seasoned Baked Chicken

Five-spice powder is a blend of powdered star anise, fennel, cinnamon, cloves, and peppercorns. It is especially nice with chicken.

3 tablespoons long grain rice
1 medium carrot, bias-sliced into 1-inch lengths (½ cup)
2 green onions, sliced (¼ cup)
1 small clove garlic, minced
⅓ cup water
1 tablespoon soy sauce
¼ teaspoon five-spice powder
Dash pepper
2 chicken drumsticks *or* thighs *or* ½ of a whole medium chicken breast

● Place a 15x12-inch piece of heavy foil, dull side down, in a baking pan or a shallow casserole, cupping sides slightly. Place *uncooked* rice in center. Add carrot, onions, and garlic. In a small mixing bowl combine water, soy sauce, five-spice powder, and pepper.

● Place chicken pieces in center of foil. Pour soy sauce mixture over chicken. Fold two opposite sides of foil together, then fold up ends to seal. Bake in a 375° oven for 45 to 50 minutes or till chicken is tender. Makes 1 serving.

Braised Turkey Thigh

What a convenience to cook once and have two meals! Use the remaining turkey in a soup.

¼ teaspoon ground sage *or* poultry seasoning
1 ¾- to 1¼-pound turkey thigh, skinned
1 tablespoon cooking oil
¾ cup water
2 tablespoons dry white wine
1 teaspoon instant chicken bouillon granules
1 small clove garlic, minced
1 bay leaf
1 medium carrot, cut into 1-inch pieces (½ cup)
2 green onions, sliced
2 tablespoons long grain rice
Dash paprika

● Rub sage or poultry seasoning into turkey thigh. In a medium skillet cook turkey thigh in hot oil over medium heat for 6 to 8 minutes or till brown, turning turkey occasionally. Drain off fat.

● Add water, wine, bouillon granules, garlic, and bay leaf to skillet. Cover and simmer slowly (for ¾-pound thigh allow 45 minutes and for 1¼-pound thigh allow 60 minutes).

● Add carrot pieces, onions, and *uncooked* rice. Cover and simmer for 25 to 30 minutes more or till turkey thigh is tender. Remove bay leaf. Transfer turkey mixture to a plate and sprinkle with paprika. Makes 1 serving.

Braised Lamb Shank Dinner

1 12-ounce lamb shank
1 clove garlic, split
1 tablespoon cooking oil
¼ cup chicken *or* beef broth
¼ cup dry white wine
2 fresh mint leaves, minced, *or* ¼ teaspoon dried mint, crushed
⅛ teaspoon dried rosemary, crushed
1 small potato, peeled and cubed (½ cup)*
 Meat Sauce (optional)

● Trim excess fat from meat. Rub lamb shank with split garlic clove. In a medium skillet cook lamb shank in hot oil over medium-high heat for 6 to 8 minutes or till brown, turning meat frequently. Place in a 10x6-inch baking dish.

● Combine broth, wine, mint, and rosemary; add to baking dish. Bake, covered, in a 350° oven for 1 hour. Add potato and bake, covered, about 30 minutes more or till potato and meat are tender. Transfer meat and potato to a plate. Serve with Meat Sauce, if desired. Makes 1 serving.

Meat Sauce: Pour liquid from baking dish into a measuring cup. Spoon off fat. If necessary, add enough *water* to liquid to make ¼ cup. Pour into a small saucepan. Combine 1 tablespoon *water* and 1 teaspoon *cornstarch;* add to liquid in saucepan. Cook and stir till thickened and bubbly. Cook and stir for 2 minutes more. Season to taste.

*You may substitute 1 medium carrot, cut into ¼-inch slices (½ cup), *or* 1 small turnip, peeled and cubed (½ cup), for the potato.

Apple-Curry Turkey Thigh

Cooking in a foil packet seals in the spicy turkey flavors and makes cleanup easy.

1 ¾- to 1¼-pound turkey thigh, skinned
¼ cup apple juice
1 small clove garlic, minced
¼ teaspoon curry powder
 Dash salt
 Dash ground red pepper
2 tablespoons long grain rice
 Dash paprika (optional)

● Place a 15x12-inch-piece of heavy foil, dull side down, in a baking pan or a shallow casserole, cupping sides slightly. Place turkey thigh in center of foil.

● In a small mixing bowl combine apple juice, garlic, curry powder, salt, and ground red pepper. Pour juice mixture over turkey. Fold two opposite sides of foil together, then fold up ends to seal. Bake in a 400° oven (for ¾-pound thigh allow 30 minutes and for 1¼-pound thigh allow 45 minutes).

● Remove from oven and open packet. Add *uncooked* rice to juice around turkey. Close packet tightly. Return to oven and bake for 25 to 30 minutes more or till turkey and rice are tender. Sprinkle with paprika, if desired. Makes 1 serving.

Italian Stuffed Chicken Breast

An elegant, easy way to serve stuffed chicken breast. You may double the recipe for company.

½ cup Fresh Tomato Sauce *
  (see recipe, page 78)
4 ounces chicken breast,
  skinned and boned
¼ cup shredded herb-
  flavored Havarti *or* Swiss
  cheese (1 ounce)
1 tablespoon fine dry bread
  crumbs
1 teaspoon grated Parmesan
  cheese
¼ teaspoon dried oregano,
  crushed
1 teaspoon margarine *or*
  butter, melted
  Hot cooked rice

● Prepare Fresh Tomato Sauce and set aside.

● Place chicken breast, boned side up, between 2 pieces of clear plastic wrap. Working from the center to the edges, pound chicken with a meat mallet to about ⅛-inch thickness. Place shredded cheese on chicken piece. Fold in sides of chicken and roll up. Press to seal.

● In a small mixing bowl stir together crumbs, Parmesan cheese, and oregano. Brush chicken with margarine or butter, then roll it in crumb mixture.

● Place chicken, seam side down, in a small shallow baking dish. Bake in a 350° oven for 30 minutes. Remove from oven. Spoon Fresh Tomato Sauce around chicken in baking dish. Bake about 10 minutes more or till chicken is tender and sauce is heated through. Serve with hot cooked rice. Makes 1 serving.

* You may substitute canned Italian-style tomato sauce for Fresh Tomato Sauce.

Turkey Skillet Supreme

Many new forms of fresh turkey are available in the grocery store. This dish uses a turkey breast slice.

4 ounces turkey breast slice
  (cut ¼ inch thick)
1 medium carrot, shredded
2 green onions, sliced
1 tablespoon margarine *or*
  butter
⅓ cup water
1 tablespoon dry Marsala *or*
  white wine
2 teaspoons all-purpose
  flour
½ teaspoon instant chicken
  bouillon granules
  Dash dried tarragon,
  crushed

● Cut turkey breast slice into ½-inch strips.

● In a medium skillet cook turkey, carrot, and onions in margarine or butter about 5 minutes or till turkey is tender and vegetables are crisp-tender. Combine water, Marsala or white wine, flour, bouillon granules, and tarragon; add to skillet.

● Cook and stir till thickened and bubbly, then cook and stir for 1 minute more. Makes 1 serving.

Cook Once, Enjoy Twice

It's great to be organized—to plan ahead and have things ready when you need them. Cooking for one can be much easier with a little planning.

Take time to plan a series of several meals. Prepare extra amounts of some foods in the first meal that can be enjoyed in a slightly different form the next time you eat. With a few minutes spent in thinking through your meals for the week, you literally cook once and enjoy twice.

Be sure to wrap the remaining portions of cooked food and refrigerate as soon as possible for the next meal.

FIRST MEAL	SECOND MEAL
Prepare *Braised Turkey Thigh* or *Apple-Curry Turkey Thigh* (see recipes, pages 70 and 71). Cook two portions of vegetables and rice. Make a lettuce salad, adding a tomato half, diced. Prepare *Refrigerator Pecan Cookie Dough* (see recipe, page 86). Bake several cookies for dessert; bake the cookie cup (see recipe, page 89) for second meal.	Use remaining cooked turkey, vegetables, and rice for *Turkey-Rice Soup* (see recipe, page 34). Or, combine the cooked turkey with remaining tomato half, diced, and spoon into a pita round for a sandwich. Heat the vegetables and rice for side dishes. Use the baked cookie cup for *Cookie-Cup Ice-Cream Sundae* (see recipe, page 89).
Prepare *Braised Lamb Shank Dinner* (see recipe, page 71) using parsnips or potatoes. Serve with a lettuce salad; add crisp raw vegetables. Cut a slice of pound cake (purchased) for dessert.	Substitute remaining cooked lamb for beef and prepare *Marinated Beef Salad* (see recipe, page 32). Or, spoon the cooked lamb into a pita round for a sandwich. Use any remaining cooked vegetables in *Cream of Any-Vegetable Soup* (see recipe, page 80). For dessert, make a trifle using a pound cake slice spread with jam and topped with whipped cream.
Prepare *Glazed Ham Slice with Sweet Potatoes* (see recipe, page 46), except bake a few extra ounces of ham. Serve with cooked broccoli (prepare an extra ¼ cup). Prepare *Basic Refrigerator Bran Muffin Batter* (see recipe, page 90) and bake a few muffins.	Prepare *Omelet for One* (see recipe, page 23); fill with remaining ham and broccoli. Serve with breadsticks or toast. For dessert, enjoy one of the muffins with *Butter Sauce* (see recipe, page 84).

The Rest of the Meal

Add that something special to a lunch or dinner with salad dressings, side dishes, sauces, desserts, and more. A recipe from The Rest of the Meal chapter could well become the star of the meal.

A Bake Shop in Your Refrigerator or Freezer

Who can resist the wonderful aroma of muffins or cookies baking in the oven. It can all begin with a muffin batter in your refrigerator and rolls of refrigerator cookie dough in your freezer. We have created six recipes using the Basic Refrigerator Bran Muffin Batter and four recipes using the Refrigerator Pecan Cookie Dough. Treat yourself to your own bake shop.

Versatile Basics

Getting down to basic recipes is where good cooking begins. The basics in this chapter begin with a simple recipe, then broaden to include variations using different flavorings and ingredients. Cream of Any-Vegetable Soup works with a variety of cooked vegetables. Make Tartar Sauce, Béarnaise-Style Sauce, or Thousand Island Dressing from Tangy Blender Mayonnaise or a variety of salad dressings from the Basic Vinaigrette.

Fruit Fits Any Meal

Not only does fruit fit any meal, but it can be a refreshing snack anytime. We have created a Fruit Compote that stores nicely in the refrigerator for as long as five days. The kinds of fruit you choose are important, too. Pink or white grapefruit, oranges, pineapple, and red or green grapes have the right texture and keeping quality. Add more perishable fruits such as apple pieces, strawberries, blueberries, and peaches to a portion at serving time. Try the Rosy Fruit Compote and choose your favorite.

'Emergency Shelf' Cooking

Too tired to cook? Not enough time to prepare recipes? Unexpected company? These are times for magic—the kind of magic you'll find in your kitchen if you stock an "emergency shelf" for last-minute cooking. It can be a corner of your pantry shelf, refrigerator, or freezer, where you keep a few quick-to-fix foods that make a meal or a snack. Start with some of the ideas below and then add to your supply as you notice products that fit your needs.

ON SHELF

Bean dip: use in Mexican Chicken Salad (page 61).

Biscuit mix

Canned chicken, tuna, or deviled ham: for sandwiches or soups. Use chicken in Gingered Chicken Salad (page 32).

Canned stew, chili: add any leftover cooked vegetables.

Cheese spread: use for a quick cheese sauce or toss with pasta.

Instant bouillon granules: great for beverages or soups. Use for broth.

Instant flavored coffee powder: for dessert beverages.

Instant soup mixes (single serving)

Italian-style tomato sauce

Microwave popcorn

Spaghetti sauce: use for Quick Pizza Tostada or Quick One-Pot Spaghetti and Meatballs (pages 38 and 51).

Steak sauce: good with meats, french fries, and Zesty Baked Potato Skins (page 33).

IN REFRIGERATOR

Bacon pieces: also try pepperoni- and ham-flavored pieces. Handy for salads, sandwiches, and toppings.

Basic Refrigerator Bran Muffin Batter: (page 90).

Refrigerator Pecan Cookie Dough: (page 86).

Soft-style cream cheese: use in Whipped Cheese Topping (page 85).

Yogurt: for Breakfast Yogurt (page 14) or snacks, or serve with fruit or pound cake.

IN FREEZER

Basic Ground Beef Mixture: (page 40).

English muffins: use for sandwiches, mini pizzas, or toast, or top with melted cheese and bacon pieces. Use in Breakfast Sandwiches to Go (pages 20 and 21).

Fresh Tomato Sauce: (page 78).

Frozen entrées: convenient to heat in microwave or toaster oven.

Frozen pound cake: for quick desserts. Serve with pudding, whipped topping, or flavored yogurt.

Nuts: use for snacks or toppings, or add to muffins, pancakes, or waffles.

Puff pastry dough: make quick shells for main dishes or cut into squares for desserts.

Refrigerator Pecan Cookie Dough: (page 86).

Toast cups: (page 47).

Fruit Compote

Make this tangy fruit compote and store it in your refrigerator for as long as five days.

1 grapefruit
¼ teaspoon finely shredded orange *or* lemon peel (set aside)
2 oranges
3 tablespoons sugar
2 teaspoons cornstarch
2 teaspoons lemon juice
⅛ teaspoon ground cardamom
Dash ground nutmeg
¾ cup fresh *or* canned pineapple chunks, drained
½ cup seedless grapes, halved
Toasted coconut *or* fresh mint leaves (optional)

● Peel and section grapefruit and oranges, reserving fruit juices. Set fruit aside.

● For sauce, add enough water to juices to make ½ cup liquid. In a small saucepan stir together juice liquid, sugar, cornstarch, lemon juice, cardamom, nutmeg, and orange or lemon peel. Cook and stir over medium heat till thickened and bubbly. Cook and stir for 2 minutes more. Cover and chill.

● In a medium mixing bowl combine grapefruit and orange sections, pineapple chunks, and grapes. Pour sauce over fruit and toss gently to coat. Cover and chill for up to 5 days. Top with toasted coconut or mint leaves, if desired. Makes 2½ cups.

Rosy Fruit Compote: Prepare Fruit Compote as directed above, *except* add 1 teaspoon *red cinnamon candies* to sauce mixture before cooking. Continue as directed.

Frozen Orange Cup

A make-ahead dessert that's ready in your freezer.

1 orange
¼ cup whipping cream*
1 teaspoon sugar*
1 tablespoon finely crushed cookie, candy bar, *or* miniature semisweet chocolate pieces (optional)

● Slice off upper ⅓ of orange. Carefully remove and drain pulp; reserve juice for another use. Reserve orange cup. Cut pulp into bite-size pieces; set aside.

● In a small mixer bowl beat cream and sugar till stiff peaks form. Fold in orange pulp and crushed cookie, candy, or chocolate pieces, if desired. Spoon into orange cup. Cover with clear plastic wrap and freeze about 3 hours or till firm. Let stand at room temperature for 15 to 20 minutes before serving. Makes 1 serving.

* You may substitute ½ cup frozen whipped dessert topping, thawed, for the whipping cream and sugar.

Fresh Tomato Sauce

½ cup chopped onion
1 small clove garlic, minced
1 tablespoon cooking oil
3 medium tomatoes, peeled and chopped (3 cups)
½ teaspoon dried Italian seasoning, crushed
½ teaspoon sugar

● In a large saucepan cook onion and garlic in oil till onion is tender. Stir in tomatoes, seasoning, sugar, ¼ teaspoon *salt,* and dash *pepper.* Simmer, uncovered, about 20 minutes or till thickened and bubbly, stirring occasionally. Use 1 portion right away and/or freeze portions for later use. Makes about two ½-cup portions.

Note: One portion of this easy sauce is used in Speedy Beef Casserole, Spanish-Style Fish Fillet, and Italian Stuffed Chicken Breast (see recipes, pages 47, 59, and 72).

Basic Vinaigrette

¼ cup salad oil
2 tablespoons vinegar
½ teaspoon dried basil, tarragon, *or* thyme, crushed, *or* dillweed
¼ teaspoon prepared mustard
Dash sugar

● In a screw-top jar combine oil, vinegar, desired herb, mustard, sugar, 2 tablespoons *water,* dash *salt,* and dash *pepper.* Cover and shake well.

● To store, refrigerate, tightly covered. Shake again before serving. Makes ½ cup.

Tartar Sauce

Basic Vinaigrette

Creamy Nutmeg-Carrot Soup
(see recipe, page 80)

Tangy Blender Mayonnaise

If you've never made mayonnaise, you're in for a surprise. It's easy, delicious, and the base for other sauces.

1   cup salad oil
1   egg
2   tablespoons white wine
      vinegar *or* lemon juice
2   teaspoons Dijon-style
      mustard
¼   teaspoon salt
      Dash pepper

● In a blender container combine ¼ *cup* oil, egg, vinegar or lemon juice, mustard, salt, and pepper. Cover and blend for 5 seconds. Through the opening in the lid, and with the blender on slow speed, *gradually* add remaining oil in a thin stream. (When necessary, stop blender and scrape sides.) To store, refrigerate, tightly covered, up to 1 month. Makes about 1¼ cups.

Tartar Sauce: Stir together ¼ cup *Tangy Blender Mayonnaise*, 1 teaspoon snipped *parsley*, 1 teaspoon drained *sweet pickle relish*, and 1 teaspoon finely chopped *onion*.

Béarnaise-Style Sauce: Stir together ¼ cup *Tangy Blender Mayonnaise*, 1 teaspoon finely chopped *green onion*, and ⅛ teaspoon *dried tarragon*, crushed.

Thousand Island Dressing: Stir together ¼ cup *Tangy Blender Mayonnaise*, 1 teaspoon *catsup or chili sauce*, 1 teaspoon finely chopped *green pepper*, and 1 teaspoon chopped *green onion*.

Watercress Sauce
(see recipe, page 81)

Fresh Tomato Sauce

Cream of Any-Vegetable Soup

A terrific way to use leftover cooked vegetables.

1 tablespoon chopped celery
1 tablespoon chopped onion
1 tablespoon margarine *or* butter
2 teaspoons all-purpose flour
¼ teaspoon instant chicken bouillon granules
Dash salt
Dash pepper
1 cup milk
Dash Worcestershire sauce
½ cup desired cooked vegetable

● In a heavy small saucepan cook celery and onion in margarine or butter till tender. Stir in flour, bouillon granules, salt, and pepper till blended. Add milk and Worcestershire sauce all at once. Cook and stir till thickened and bubbly, then cook and stir for 1 minute more.

● Cool slightly; place vegetable and milk mixture in a blender container. Cover and blend about 30 seconds or till smooth. Return to saucepan and heat through. Makes 1 serving.

Creamy Nutmeg-Carrot Soup: Prepare Cream of Any-Vegetable Soup as directed above using cooked *carrots, except* add dash ground *nutmeg* before blending.

Cheesy Cauliflower Soup: Prepare Cream of Any-Vegetable Soup as directed above using cooked *cauliflower, except* add 1 tablespoon grated *Parmesan cheese* and dash *garlic salt* before blending. Top with chopped parsley.

Curried Broccoli Soup: Prepare Cream of Any-Vegetable Soup as directed above using cooked *broccoli, except* add dash *curry powder* before blending.

Minted Green Pea Soup: Prepare Cream of Any-Vegetable Soup as directed above using cooked *peas, except* add dash dried *mint leaves*, crushed, before blending.

Creamy Mushroom Soup with Chives: Prepare Cream of Any-Vegetable Soup as directed above using cooked *mushrooms*. Top with 1 teaspoon snipped *chives*.

Dilled Potato Soup: Prepare Cream of Any-Vegetable Soup as directed above using cooked *potato, except* add ¼ teaspoon dried *dillweed* before blending.

Creamy Tarragon-Spinach Soup: Prepare Cream of Any-Vegetable Soup as directed above using cooked *spinach, except* add ⅛ to ¼ teaspoon dried *tarragon*, crushed, before blending.

Basic White Sauce

One sauce becomes many different sauces with the addition of flavoring ingredients.

1 tablespoon margarine *or* butter
1 tablespoon all-purpose flour
Dash salt
Dash pepper
1 cup milk

● In a heavy small saucepan melt margarine or butter. Stir in flour, salt, and pepper till blended. Add milk all at once. Cook and stir over medium heat till mixture is thickened and bubbly, then cook and stir for 1 minute more. To store, refrigerate in an airtight container for up to 4 days. Makes about 1 cup.

Note: For variety, add a little of any of the following, according to taste: snipped *chives,* ground *nutmeg, onion juice,* chopped *parsley,* dry *sherry, or Worcestershire sauce.*

Cheese Sauce: Using ¼ cup Basic White Sauce, stir in 2 tablespoons shredded *cheese (American, Colby, Swiss, or Gruyère),* dash dry *mustard,* if desired, and dash ground *nutmeg,* if desired, till cheese melts.

Herb Sauce: Using ¼ cup Basic White Sauce, stir in 1 teaspoon snipped *chives,* dash dry *mustard,* dash dried *savory,* crushed, and dash *pepper.* Add 1 tablespoon chopped fresh *watercress or parsley,* if desired.

Watercress Sauce: Using ¼ cup Basic White Sauce, stir in 1 tablespoon chopped fresh *watercress,* ¼ teaspoon *Dijon-style mustard,* and dash ground *nutmeg.* You may substitute chopped *parsley or* snipped *chives* for fresh watercress.

Wine Sauce: Using ¼ cup Basic White Sauce, stir in 1 tablespoon shredded *Gruyère cheese* and 2 teaspoons dry *sherry or* dry *white wine* till cheese melts. Season to taste.

Vegetable Stir-Fry

Oriental oyster sauce gives stir-fried vegetables an exciting taste.

1 tablespoon cooking oil
1 small carrot, sliced into ¼-inch pieces (⅓ cup)
½ small zucchini, sliced (⅓ cup)
½ sweet red, green, *or* yellow pepper, cut into ¼-inch strips (½ cup)
3 fresh mushrooms, sliced
1 green onion, bias-sliced into 1-inch lengths
2 teaspoons oyster sauce *or* soy sauce
    Dash garlic powder

● Preheat a medium skillet over medium-high heat; add oil. Add carrot pieces and stir-fry for 2 minutes. (Add more oil as necessary during cooking.) Add zucchini; stir-fry for 1½ to 2 minutes. Add red pepper, mushrooms, and green onion to the skillet; stir-fry about 1 minute or till vegetables are crisp-tender.

● Add oyster sauce or soy sauce and garlic powder to the skillet. Stir the vegetables till coated with sauce. Serve immediately. Makes 1 serving.

Note: When preparing vegetables for stir-fry, prepare an extra amount and make a marinated vegetable salad. In a small bowl or reclosable plastic bag combine about 1 cup sliced raw *vegetables* and 2 tablespoons Basic Vinaigrette (see recipe, page 78). Cover and store in the refrigerator for up to 3 days.

Baked Rice with Fruit and Nuts

Dried fruit bits are a new product sold in handy small packages.

½ cup hot water
¼ cup chopped apple (optional)
3 tablespoons long grain rice
1 tablespoon sliced green onion
1 tablespoon mixed dried fruit bits *or* raisins
1 tablespoon toasted slivered almonds, sunflower nuts, *or* pine nuts
1 teaspoon margarine *or* butter
½ teaspoon instant chicken bouillon granules
    Dash five-spice powder, ground cumin, *or* turmeric

● In a 10- or 12-ounce baking dish combine water, apple (if desired), *uncooked* rice, green onion, dried fruit bits or raisins, almonds, margarine or butter, bouillon granules, and five-spice powder.

● Bake, covered, in a 350° oven for 30 to 35 minutes or till rice is tender. Makes 1 serving.

Vegetable Stir-Fry

Quick Fudge Sauce

A chocolate lover's delight.

1 cup sifted powdered sugar
½ cup semisweet chocolate
    pieces*
2 tablespoons margarine *or*
    butter
2 tablespoons light corn
    syrup
2 tablespoons light cream
½ teaspoon vanilla
    Dash salt

● In a heavy small saucepan combine powdered sugar, chocolate, margarine or butter, corn syrup, cream, vanilla, and salt. Cook and stir over low heat till chocolate is melted and mixture is smooth.

● To store, refrigerate, tightly covered, for up to 2 weeks. To reheat, spoon desired amount of sauce into saucepan and heat over low heat, stirring constantly, until sauce is warm. Serve warm over ice cream, cake, or fruit. Makes 1 cup.

* For a bittersweet sauce, substitute 2 squares (2 ounces) *unsweetened chocolate,* chopped, for the semisweet chocolate pieces.

Butter Sauce

Warm this sauce and serve it over just about anything—Cranberry Loaf (see recipe, page 92), pound cake, angel food cake, ice cream, even sliced bananas.

1 cup sugar
½ cup light cream
¼ cup butter *or* margarine
1 teaspoon rum *or* 2 drops
    rum flavoring (optional)
½ teaspoon vanilla

● In a heavy small saucepan combine sugar, cream, butter or margarine, rum, if desired, and vanilla. Cook and stir over medium-high heat till boiling. Boil for 4 minutes more.

● To store, refrigerate, tightly covered, for up to 2 weeks. To reheat, spoon desired amount of sauce into saucepan and heat over low heat, stirring constantly, until sauce is warm. Serve warm. Makes 1 cup.

Butter Pecan Sauce

This sauce won't stay around for long—it's too good.

¼ cup pecan pieces
2 tablespoons butter *or* margarine
½ cup packed brown sugar
2 tablespoons light corn syrup
2 tablespoons light cream
½ teaspoon vanilla

● In a heavy small saucepan cook pecans in butter or margarine till pecans are lightly toasted. Stir in brown sugar, corn syrup, and cream. Simmer for 2 minutes; stir in vanilla.

● To store, refrigerate, tightly covered, for up to 2 weeks. To reheat, spoon desired amount of sauce into saucepan and heat over low heat, stirring constantly, until sauce is warm. Serve warm over the Dessert Waffle (see recipe, page 93), ice cream, or cake. Makes ¾ cup.

Orange Sauce

The fresh flavor of this sauce will complement many foods, such as Ginger Cake (see recipe, page 91) or baked ham.

¼ cup sugar
2 teaspoons cornstarch
½ teaspoon finely shredded orange peel
¾ cup orange juice
1 tablespoon margarine *or* butter

● In a heavy small saucepan combine sugar and cornstarch. Add orange peel, orange juice, and margarine or butter. Cook and stir over medium heat till thickened and bubbly, then cook and stir for 2 minutes more.

● To store, refrigerate, tightly covered, for up to 1 week. Serve warm or chilled. To reheat, spoon desired amount of sauce into saucepan and heat over low heat, stirring constantly, until sauce is warm. Makes about 1 cup.

Whipped Cheese Topping

Use this topping over warm gingerbread. Or spread it on sliced banana bread or between thin cookies for dessert sandwiches.

3 ounces soft-style cream cheese (⅓ cup)
3 tablespoons powdered sugar
½ teaspoon finely shredded orange peel
Milk (optional)

● In a small bowl combine cream cheese, sugar, and orange peel. Mix till well blended. To store, refrigerate, tightly covered, for up to 1 week. To serve, you may need to stir milk into the amount of topping you plan to use to make topping of desired consistency for intended use. Makes about ½ cup.

Refrigerator Pecan Cookie Dough

1¼ cups all-purpose flour
¼ teaspoon baking soda
¼ teaspoon salt
⅓ cup margarine *or* butter
½ cup sugar
¼ cup packed brown sugar
1 egg
½ teaspoon vanilla
¼ teaspoon almond extract
   (optional)
½ cup finely chopped pecans,
   toasted

● Stir together flour, baking soda, and salt; set aside. In a small mixer bowl beat margarine or butter on medium speed of an electric mixer about 30 seconds. Add sugar and brown sugar; beat till fluffy. Add egg, vanilla, and almond extract; beat well.

● Add flour mixture to creamed mixture, beating on low speed till well combined. Stir in pecans.* Chill dough for 1 hour. Shape into two 6-inch rolls and wrap tightly in waxed paper.

● Store dough in the refrigerator for up to 1 week or in the freezer for up to 6 months. Use in the recipes on pages 87, 88, and 89. Or, chill for several hours or till firm. If using margarine, you may need to chill dough in the freezer to make it firm enough to slice. Cut into ¼-inch slices and place on an ungreased cookie sheet. Bake in a 375° oven for 8 to 10 minutes or till slightly brown. Remove and cool on a wire rack. If desired, you can sandwich 2 cookies together with prepared frosting. Makes about 48 cookies.

*To make drop cookies, drop dough from a teaspoon onto an ungreased cookie sheet. If desired, flatten cookies slightly using the tines of a fork. Bake as directed.

**Cookie-Cup
Ice-Cream Sundae**
(see recipe, page 89)

Pots de Crème Tart
(see recipe, page 88)

86

Fruit Tart

Just press cookie dough into a miniature pie plate for an easy tart.

2 tablespoons Refrigerator Pecan Cookie Dough (see recipe, opposite)

¼ cup Whipped Cheese Topping (see recipe, page 85)

Fresh raspberries, fresh strawberries, sliced, *or* seedless grapes, halved

● Carefully press cookie dough into a greased 4¼x1-inch pie plate, forming ¾-inch-high sides. Bake in a 350° oven for 12 to 15 minutes or till golden brown. Cool for 5 minutes. Remove from pie plate, then cool on a wire rack.

● Meanwhile, prepare Whipped Cheese Topping; *do not* add any milk. To assemble, spread topping over cooled tart shell. Top with raspberries, strawberries, or grapes. Chill for at least 1 hour or as long as overnight (tart shell will soften during chilling). Makes 1 tart.

Refrigerator
Pecan
Cookies

Fruit Tart

Pots de Crème Tart

Pots de crème is a smooth, rich, chocolate pudding.

3 tablespoons Pots de Crème
(see recipe, below)
2 tablespoons Refrigerator
Pecan Cookie Dough (see
recipe, page 86)
Toasted sliced almonds *or*
chocolate curls

● Prepare Pots de Crème; chill till thickened. Meanwhile, carefully press cookie dough into a greased 4¼x1-inch pie plate, forming ¾-inch-high sides. Bake in a 350° oven for 12 to 15 minutes or till golden brown. Cool for 5 minutes. Remove from pie plate, then cool on a wire rack.

● To assemble, spread Pots de Crème over cooled tart shell. Top with almond slices or chocolate curls. Chill for at least 1 hour or as long as overnight (tart shell will soften during chilling). Makes 1 tart.

Pots de Crème

This Pots de crème (po-deh-KREM) recipe makes two servings because it would not be convenient to work with smaller amounts of ingredients.

⅔ cup light cream
½ cup semisweet chocolate
pieces
Dash salt (optional)
1 egg yolk, beaten
1 teaspoon rum *or* ¼
teaspoon vanilla

● In a heavy small saucepan combine cream, chocolate, and salt, if desired. Cook and stir over medium-low heat till smooth and slightly thickened. *Gradually* stir hot mixture into egg yolk. Return to saucepan. Cook and stir for 2 minutes more; stir in rum or vanilla.

● Pour into 2 serving dishes. Cover with clear plastic wrap and refrigerate overnight. Makes 2 servings.

Cookie-Cup Ice-Cream Sundae

An easy dessert to make for guests, when you have Refrigerator Pecan Cookie Dough on hand in your freezer.

Quick Fudge Sauce (see
   recipe, page 84) *or* sliced
   strawberries
5 slices Refrigerator Pecan
   Cookie Dough cut ⅛ inch
   thick (see recipe, page 86)
   Ice cream

● Prepare Quick Fudge Sauce or strawberries. Place 1 dough slice in bottom of a greased 6-ounce custard cup. Place remaining 4 dough slices against the sides of the cup, making sure slices do not touch each other. Bake in a 375° oven for 10 to 12 minutes or till slightly brown.

● Cool in cup for 2 minutes; carefully loosen sides and bottom. *Do not remove.* Continue cooling for 15 minutes. Remove from cup, then cool thoroughly on a wire rack.

● To serve, place 1 scoop ice cream in cookie cup. Top with warm Quick Fudge Sauce or strawberries. Makes 1 serving.

Making a cookie cup
Slice five ⅛-inch-thick slices from the roll of cookie dough. Place 1 slice in the bottom of the custard cup. *Do not flatten.* Place remaining four slices against the sides of the custard cup as shown, making sure petals do not touch one another.

Basic Refrigerator Bran Muffin Batter

Use this basic batter to make muffins, pancakes, a variety of dessert cakes, and even a dessert waffle.

2 cups raisin bran cereal
1 cup buttermilk
1¼ cups all-purpose flour
2 teaspoons baking powder
½ teaspoon ground cinnamon
¼ teaspoon baking soda
⅛ teaspoon salt
¾ cup sugar
¼ cup cooking oil
1 egg

● Combine raisin bran cereal and buttermilk; let stand for 5 minutes. Stir together flour, baking powder, cinnamon, baking soda, and salt. In a large mixer bowl beat sugar and oil on medium speed of electric mixer about 30 seconds. Add egg and beat till well combined. *Alternately* stir bran mixture and dry ingredients into beaten mixture just till moistened.

● Store in the refrigerator, tightly covered, for up to 2 weeks. Use in the recipes on pages 17, 91, 92, and 93. Or, spoon ⅓ cup batter into a greased 6-ounce custard cup. If desired, top with 2 thin *apple slices,* then a mixture of 1 teaspoon *brown sugar* and dash ground *cinnamon.* Bake in a 350° oven for 18 to 20 minutes or till golden. Makes 18 muffins.

Ginger Cake

Cranberry Loaf
(see recipe, page 92)

Ginger Cake

Serve the cake warm. It's an old-fashioned dessert to remember.

⅓ cup Basic Refrigerator Bran
   Muffin Batter (see recipe,
   opposite)
1 teaspoon raisins
½ teaspoon unsweetened
   cocoa powder
⅛ teaspoon ground ginger
   Whipped Cheese Topping
   (see recipe, page 85)
   (optional)
   Orange Sauce (see recipe,
   page 85)

● In a small mixing bowl gently fold together batter, raisins, cocoa powder, and ginger. Spoon into a greased 3½-inch individual tube pan.* Bake in a 350° oven for 15 to 17 minutes or till a wooden toothpick inserted in center comes out clean. Cool for 5 minutes; remove from pan.

● To serve, spoon Whipped Cheese Topping on top of cake, if desired, and drizzle with Orange Sauce. Makes 1 tiny cake.

*If an individual tube pan is not available, use a greased 4½x2½x1½-inch pan; bake in a 350° oven for 15 to 17 minutes. *Or,* use a greased 6-ounce custard cup; bake in a 350° oven for 20 to 22 minutes.

Carrot Cake
(see recipe, page 92)

Butter Pecan Sauce
(see recipe, page 85)

Dessert Waffle
(see recipe, page 93)

**Basic Refrigerator
Bran Muffins**

C a r r o t Cake

The popular carrot cake made so easy with on-hand Basic Refrigerator Bran Muffin Batter.

⅓ cup Basic Refrigerator Bran Muffin Batter (see recipe, page 90)
2 tablespoons finely shredded carrot
1 teaspoon wheat germ *or* wheat bran
¼ teaspoon vanilla
¼ cup Whipped Cheese Topping (see recipe, page 85)
Toasted coconut (optional)

● In a small mixing bowl gently fold together batter, carrot, wheat germ or wheat bran, and vanilla. Spoon into a greased 6-ounce custard cup. Bake in a 350° oven for 25 to 30 minutes or till a wooden toothpick inserted in center comes out clean. Cool for 5 minutes. Remove from cup, then cool on a wire rack.

● Prepare Whipped Cheese Topping. To assemble, slice cake in half horizontally. Fill and frost top with topping. Sprinkle with toasted coconut, if desired. Makes 1 serving.

Cranberry Loaf

Keep cranberries in your freezer so you can bake this loaf all year long.

1¼ cups Basic Refrigerator Bran Muffin Batter (see recipe, page 90)
¼ cup fresh *or* frozen cranberries
1 tablespoon wheat germ *or* wheat bran
Butter Sauce (see recipe, page 84)

● In a small mixing bowl gently fold together batter, cranberries, and wheat germ or wheat bran. Spoon into a greased 5½x3½x2-inch loaf pan. Bake in a 350° oven for 45 to 50 minutes or till a wooden toothpick inserted in center comes out clean. Cool for 10 minutes. Remove from pan, then cool thoroughly on a wire rack.

● Meanwhile, prepare Butter Sauce. To serve, drizzle sauce over a slice of Cranberry Loaf. Makes 1 small loaf.

Dessert Waffle

A great finish for a light soup or salad meal.

Butter Pecan Sauce (see recipe, page 85)
½ cup Basic Refrigerator Bran Muffin Batter (see recipe, page 90)
2 tablespoons milk
1 tablespoon chopped nuts
1 teaspoon cooking oil
Fresh *or* thawed, frozen peach slices (optional)
Ice cream (optional)
Whipped cream (optional)

● Prepare Butter Pecan Sauce and keep warm. In a small mixing bowl combine batter, milk, nuts, and oil. Stir just till mixed; *do not overmix.*

● Pour batter onto grids of a preheated, well-greased waffle baker. Close lid quickly; do not open during baking. Use a fork to help lift the baked waffle off grid.

● To serve, spoon peaches, ice cream, and/or whipped cream on waffle, if desired. Drizzle with Butter Pecan Sauce. Makes 1 waffle.

Banana-Rum Dessert

Many restaurants serve this dessert flaming and call it Bananas Foster.

1 tablespoon margarine *or* butter
½ teaspoon finely shredded orange peel
1 tablespoon brown sugar
1 tablespoon orange juice
1 medium banana
1 tablespoon dark rum, orange liqueur, *or* banana liqueur
Ice cream *or* whipped cream (optional)

● In a small skillet melt margarine or butter. Stir in orange peel, brown sugar, and orange juice. Slice banana lengthwise and quarter; add to skillet. Cook over medium heat for 2 minutes. Stir in rum or liqueur; coat banana with sauce. Cook for 1 to 2 minutes more or till sauce is thickened and bubbly.

● Serve with ice cream or whipped cream, if desired. Makes 1 serving.

Index

Index

You may be cooking for
yourself and occasionally
dieting, too. If so, then turn to
BETTER HOMES AND
GARDENS® *Dieting for One.*
Choose from 90 easy, lower-
in-calorie recipes that
make dieting and cooking for
one fun.